D0357981

HENCEFORWARD . . .

by the same author

A CHORUS OF DISAPPROVAL
WOMAN IN MIND
A SMALL FAMILY BUSINESS

HENCEFORWARD . . .

ALAN AYCKBOURN

faber and faber
LONDON · BOSTON

First published in 1988
by Faber and Faber Limited
3 Queen Square London WCIN 3AU

Photoset by Wilmaset Birkenhead Wirral
Printed in Great Britain by
Cox & Wyman Ltd Reading Berks
All rights reserved

All rights whatsoever in this play are strictly
reserved and applications for permission to perform it,
etc., must be made in advance, before rehearsals begin, to
Margaret Ramsay Ltd, 14a Goodwin Court, St Martins Lane,
London WC2N 4LL

British Library Cataloguing in Publication Data

Ayckbourn, Alan, 1939–
Henceforward —
I. Title
822'.914
ISBN 0–571–15185–X

CHARACTERS

JEROME   a composer
CORINNA   his wife
GEAIN   their daughter
ZOË   an actress
MERVYN   a welfare officer
NAN 300F
LUPUS
YOUNG GEAIN   } (*Video only*)

Note
NAN 300F is played by the same actress as CORINNA in Act I and by the same actress as ZOË in Act II.

Scene: Jerome's studio.

Act I: Friday night/Saturday morning. Sometime quite soon.
Act II: A few days later.

Henceforward . . . was first performed in Scarborough at the Stephen Joseph Theatre in the Round on 30 July 1987. The cast was as follows:

JEROME	Barry McCarthy
LUPUS	Robin Herford
ZOË	Serena Evans
GEAIN, aged nine	Victoria Horsfield
GEAIN, aged thirteen	Emma Chambers
CORINNA	Penny Bunton
MERVYN	Michael Roberts

It was subsequently performed at the Vaudeville Theatre, London, on 16 November 1988. The cast was as follows:

JEROME	Ian McKellen
LUPUS	Robin Herford
ZOË	Serena Evans
GEAIN, aged nine	Victoria Horsfield
GEAIN, aged thirteen	Emma Chambers
CORINNA	Jane Asher
MERVYN	Michael Simkins

Notes on the Music

Paul Todd's music which was used in both the Scarborough and West End productions of *Henceforward* . . . is available for hire from Margaret Ramsay Limited on cassette tape. Should the production require the actual voices of an individual company this, too, can be arranged through Margaret Ramsay Limited. Care should be exercised in attempting special composition: the original score was constructed on a Synclavier, and the text requires an instrument of similar sophistication.

ACT I

SCENE I

A darkened living room of a flat. The only light is from a video/ sound console system, at present inactive. We can make out very little or guess the time of day. All at once, a large wall-mounted video screen lights up. Or perhaps a series of screens. We see the picture as from a front-door video entryphone system. JEROME, *a man of about forty, can be seen at the door. He is carrying three carrier bags, together with a somewhat incongruous walking stick. We see* JEROME *inserting his key and struggling and muttering as he opens his front door. He enters the flat. As he closes the front door the screen blanks again. After a second, the hall lights come on and* JEROME *approaches down the hall. Then the lights come on in the living area.*

It's a curious room. No windows, or, at least, what there were are curtained off and no light comes through the heavy steel shutters outside. There is a sofa, two swivel chairs and a low coffee-type table – all modern. That's really the extent of the recognizable furniture. The remainder of the room is filled with some very sophisticated electronic equipment. Not an amateur electronic rat's nest of wire and cable but custom-built units containing computers, tape and disc recorders – racks of amplifiers, filters, reverb units and gismos of all descriptions. At one end, several keyboards. Some of these are covered and remain so until much later in the play when we realize for the first time what a vast array of equipment JEROME *actually owns. The room, in fact, betrays the contradictions in his own character. For while the immaculate technical equipment is kept lovingly protected from the slightest speck of dust, the rest of the room – the living area – is in fair chaos. Remnants of instant meals, old tea and coffee cups, the odd item of clothing. The signs of someone who lives alone and has stopped caring much. And, strangely, the overall impression given off, despite all the modern paraphernalia, is of something faintly Gothic. Three ways off, one to the hall and front door, one to the kitchen and one to the rest of the flat – the bedrooms, bathroom, etc.*

JEROME *is standing in the hall doorway having just switched on the lights. He dumps his packages on the sofa and replaces his stick near the hall doorway. Also on the sofa, slumped, face down in a somewhat undignified posture is* NAN, *who remains motionless for some time.* JEROME, *ignoring her, crosses to the console, where he switches on his answering machine. As he moves back to the sofa, on the screen and through the speakers, the machine fast-rewinds. He doesn't take much notice of it, though. He gathers up two of the carriers which appear to be filled with tinfoil-sealed instant meals and goes off into the kitchen. As he does so, the answering machine starts to play back both sound and vision. An introductory beep. A logo appears:* The Department of Social Services. ECONOMY. Except in special circumstances all calls made are NVR. 01–993–9000.

MERVYN'S VOICE: Mr Watkins, this is Mervyn Bickerdyke
from the Department of Child Wellbeing . . .
(JEROME *groans.*)
I've been trying to get hold of you for some days now,
regarding a meeting. The time is nine forty-six. I wonder if
you would call me. My number is on screen. Thank you.
(*He hangs up. The screen blanks, the audio beeps. In a second, the next message appears.*)

JEROME: (*On his way to the kitchen, in reply to* MERVYN) No, I
won't and I'm not.
(*A fanfare-like tune from the answering machine and a logo appears:* BLAISE GILLESPIE – Escorts for the Discerning.)

CHOIR: (*Singing, from the video*) Blaise Gillespie! A call from
Blaise Gillespie!

VOICE: (*Cheerfully*) Hallo, Mr Watkins, this is Mary Hope-
Fitch, calling once again from the Blaise Gillespie Agency.
It's ten-forty on Thursday. Just to remind you of your
appointment today with Zoë Mill who plans to be with you
by fourteen hundred this afternoon. I hope that's still
convenient. She's looking forward so much to meeting you.
We feel certain she'll answer all your rather specialized
requirements. If there's any problem at all, please don't
hesitate to call. Thank you.
(JEROME *returns from the kitchen for his third carrier bag.*)

CHOIR: (*Singing, from the video*) Blaise Gillespie! A call from
Blaise Gillespie . . .

2

JEROME: (*Mimicking them*) From tone-deaf Blaise Gillespie . . .
(*Another couple of beeps as the message ends and moves on to the next. It is the same logo as the first call.*)

MERVYN'S VOICE: Mr Watkins, this is Mervyn Bickerdyke, Department of Child Wellbeing . . .
(JEROME *groans. And goes into the kitchen with the carrier.*)
It is urgent that I speak to you. I realize you may be – busy with your compositions – but it is a matter of some importance. It's eleven seventeen and my number is on screen. Thank you.
(JEROME *returns with one of the tinfoil food packages in one hand, a palm-sized section of printed circuitry in the other. A beep as the message ends on the answering machine.*)

JEROME: Look what I've brought for you. (*He balances the circuitry casually on* NAN's *back as he passes her.*) Who's a spoilt girl, then?
(JEROME *sits on the sofa and studies his purchase. Another beep. The screen crackles and flickers with a fuzzy image that could be anyone's.*)

ZOË'S VOICE: (*Faintly*) Hello, this is Zoë Mill. I'm from the Blaise Gillespie Agency. And it's eleven fifteen . . . Hallo? Hallo, this is Zoë . . . Hallo? Can you hear me? Oh, dammit . . .
(*Another beep. The screen clears.* JEROME, *unperturbed, continues to read. Another beep. Interference as before, if not worse.*)
Hallo, this is . . . Oh, Jesus! Don't any of these bloody things work at . . . ?
(*Another beep as* ZOË *is cut off.* JEROME *reads on. As he does so, there is a swift beep – a yell from* ZOË *and another beep – qualifying as the shortest message ever.*)
(*In fury*) Aaarrrgggh!
(*From the machine, another beep and* LUPUS *appears on the screen. He is a forlorn sight, a harassed, careworn man in his forties. He wears a T-shirt reading MUSIC IS A LIVING THING. It appears he is at home, from the background we can see behind him. The sound of a child playing out of sight.*)

3

LUPUS: Hallo, Jerry. It's me. Lupus. I thought I'd just call
you, mate . . .
(JEROME, *reacting to* LUPUS's *voice, gives a terrible groan.*)
. . . keep you up to date with how things are –
(*A ball, presumably thrown by a child, bounces off* LUPUS's
head. The CHILD *laughs.*)
(*Ineffectually*) Ah, now don't do that, Orson . . . That hurt
Daddy. The point is, Jerry, it's come to the big N.C.H.
Ultimatums from Deborah. Threats from the Bank
Manager. I mean real threats, Jerry. Two heavy lads in
camel-hair coats kicking at my front door. So it looks like
I'm going to have to take that job with those geriatrics. I
never thought it would get this desperate, Jerry. Look at
me, I'm a top session-player –
(*He is struck again by a projectile.*)
Orson – don't do that, darling, Daddy's talking – Jesus –
what am I reduced to – ? – relief drummer in a three-piece
band for an old folks' dance in Finchley. Who needs it,
Jerry? Answer. I need it. Desperately I need it.
(JEROME, *apparently following the instructions he has been
studying, removes the tinfoil package from its sleeve and
searches for an insulated surface. In the end he decides to place
the container on one of his discarded items of clothing, a shirt,
which he spreads on the coffee table.*)
My God, I do. Because there's nothing else. But I don't
have to tell you.
(JEROME, *having positioned his container, holds it in one
hand, and tugs at a red ring in the lid. This pulls out a length
of metal strip which he is left holding in his other hand. He
stares at both items suspiciously.* JEROME, *during the next, goes
to the answering machine, tossing aside the packet.*)
And if Deborah leaves me, Jerry, which it looks as if she's
going to – it's sorting out the suitcases time, you know –
but if Deborah goes – on top of everything else . . . I
mean, I've been a loving husband. I've been a forgiving
husband. God, have I been forgiving? I let her play around
with – every bastard who could make it up our stairs.
Present company excepted. I just don't know what I'm

4

going to do, old mate . . .

(JEROME *pushes a button on the console and* LUPUS *goes into fast-forward mode. He spools jerkily on for some time. The odd child-aimed missile hits him on the head as his high-speed voice twitters on.* JEROME *finishes his instructions. He shrugs and moves over to* NAN, *picks up the printed circuit card and examines it. He goes to a cupboard beneath the console and gets out a large loose-leaf manual. He studies this. As he does so,* LUPUS's *message on the tape ends, the machine beeps and resumes normal speed. Another beep. The screen reads:* FAULT: VISION TEMPORARILY INOPERATIVE.)

ZOË'S VOICE: (*Rather distraught*) Hallo. This is Zoë Mill from the Blaise Gillespie Agency at – God, what's the time? – it's twelve thirty-one – All right? I've been trying to phone you for ages – Only none of the – And I keep getting your machine. My train is – my *bloody* train – pardon the language – is delayed – and I'm now at – God knows where I am – Oh, where the hell am I? Just hold on a second.

(*Station sounds as, apparently, she opens the call-box door.*)

(*Calling to someone*) Excuse me! I say, excuse me. Could you tell me where I am, please? . . . Where? . . . Hendon Central? Thanks so much.

(*Door closes.*)

Hallo, I'm at a place called Hendon Central, apparently. So I don't know when I'll reach you. More important, I hope you're there because I'd hate to think I –

(*She is interrupted by a series of beeps.*)

Oh, I've no more on my card, that's it. See you shortly. I hope. Otherwise I –

(*The screen goes dead and then reads:* MESSAGES END.

JEROME *remains impervious to this. He is still intently studying the manual. After a second, the screen blanks.*)

JEROME: (*At length*) All right. Let's see what we can do.

(*He rather unceremoniously puts his hand up the back of* NAN's *skirt and fumbles for a moment.*)

Pardon me.

(*There is a click and his hand re-emerges with an identical piece*

5

of printed circuitry.)

Ah-ha!

(*He studies it critically for a moment and then throws it aside. His hand goes back under her dress as he replaces the circuit with the new piece. There is a series of clicks.*)

(*As he does so*) Now . . . I'm not supposed to be doing this, you know . . . If they caught me doing this . . . they'd . . . aaah! . . . get in . . . they'd probably lock me up and melt you down for scrap . . . I had to steal this from a check-out machine at the supermarket when their backs were . . . aah!

(*A final click.*)

NAN: (*A little sigh*) Aaah!

JEROME: Ah! There you go. Good girl. Now.

(*He heaves* NAN *round and sits her up on the sofa.*)

God, you're a heavy old bag of bits. Come on.

(*He grabs her neck on either side brings it sharply forward and then back.* NAN *clicks. A male voice, decidedly not hers, probably a long forgotten technician's, emanates from somewhere in* NAN.)

VOICE: NAN 300F, series four, model 99148622G for Gertie. System check commencing – Go.

(NAN *goes through her pre-check routine. This is rapid and comprehensive. A great deal of internal computer chatter as systems load. Her eyes blink rapidly, her mouth flaps, every joint of her body tenses then relaxes. She rises, sits, her limbs jerk.*)

NAN: (*In her own voice, very rapidly*) Modified Sampling Commences. Oh–for–God's–sake–Jerome–can't–you– think–of–anyone–else–but–yourself–for–a–change–just– for–once–I–mean–what–sort–of–a–person–are–you? Modified Sampling Ends.

(*A few more whirrs and clicks.*)

System check complete. Operational eighty-three point one seven. We are sixteen point eight three per cent unstable and are within eight point one seven per cent of permanent shutdown. (*Cheerfully*) Clock set o-eight-hundred hours. Good morning. Rise and shine.

6

JEROME: Nan, walk about.

NAN: Walk about, Nan.

(She does so. She walks with a rather bouncy stride but has a slight limp. She clanks a little as she goes down on her bad leg. JEROME watches her critically as she circles a couple of times.)

JEROME: That's better. You're not bumping into things like you were. I've still got to fix your leg, though. It's the pivot. You need a new pivot, old girl. Only they've stopped making them, you see.

NAN: *(Banging into a piece of furniture)* Oh, for goodness' sake, you extremely stupid old bat. Who put that there, then? *(This last reveals the slightly tetchier side of NAN. In fact, as time goes on, we see that she is rather a Jekyll-and-Hyde creature. Her sunnier nature is the result of her initial 'nanny' factory programming; her darker side the result of subsequent modifications by JEROME himself – the source of which will become clearer later.)*

JEROME: Nan, come here.

NAN: Coming, Nan.

(NAN comes to him and stops in front of him.)

JEROME: That's it.

(JEROME crouches down and lifts her skirt to examine her knee. We see that at the knee joint her legs cease to be humanoid and are exposed metalwork. NAN licks her fingers and starts to smooth JEROME's hair.)

NAN: That's better . . .

JEROME: Don't do that . . .

NAN: That's better.

JEROME: Nan, stop.

NAN: Stop, Nan.

(NAN stops. He rises.)

JEROME: Nan, watch my finger.

NAN: Watching your finger, Nan.

(He moves his finger to and fro in front of her eyes. She follows it with her eyes very slowly.)

JEROME: Yes, I think we can sharpen your reflexes a bit.

(He places his hand inside NAN's blouse while continuing to move his other hand in front of her eyes. NAN's response

7

quickens noticeably.)

That's it . . . that's better . . .

(NAN *suddenly twitches violently.*)

Whoops! Too much. Sorry. That's it. Nan, thank you.

NAN: Thank you. Lovely glass of orange? Lovely orange?

JEROME: Nan, lovely.

NAN: Lovely. Lovely morning. Rise and shine.

(*She bounces off to the kitchen.*)

JEROME: (*Glancing at his watch*) Oh, I never set your clock, did I? Never mind. You're better than you were.

(*He goes to the console and plays with a few switches. From the kitchen a crash.*)

NAN: (*Off*) Oh, for goodness' sake, you extremely stupid old bat. Who put that there, then?

(JEROME *frowns but ingnores the sound. He puts on some Bach. It relaxes him. The phone rings. He makes no effort to answer it. It continues to ring.*)

JEROME: Go away, Lupus, I'm not here.

(*He notices suddenly that his meal is still sitting there in its tinfoil.*)

Oh, no!

(*He grabs hold of the tinfoil package. It is very hot.*)

(*Dropping it*) Ah!

(*He picks it up with the shirt it was standing on and cautiously, still protecting his hands, he opens the lid. The contents are black and charred and smoking.*)

(*Disgustedly*) Oh, miraculous.

(*He drops the tinfoil back on the table.* NAN *comes in with a mug in her hand. It is unfortunately empty since she is holding it upside down.*)

NAN: (*Placing the inverted mug on the table by* JEROME) Lovely glass of orange. (*Heading towards the bedrooms*) Lovely morning, wakey-wakey.

JEROME: (*Staring at the mug in disgust*) You load of old scrap.

(*He is about to drop the shirt, too, when he observes that it now has a burn mark on it, left from the heated tinfoil.*)

(*Equally*) Oh, mind-numbing.

(*He lies on the sofa for a moment absorbing the music.* NAN *re-*

8

enters with a face flannel in her hand. She makes a beeline for JEROME.)

NAN: (*Playfully*) Booo! Nan's coming to getcher!
(NAN *attacks his face vigorously with a flannel.* JEROME *struggles. She is apparently quite strong.*)

JEROME: Waah! Noff.

NAN: Come along, wash your face and hands before your breakfast!

JEROME: Wah! Noff! (*Getting his mouth clear*) Nan off! Nan off!
(NAN *stops at once.*)

NAN: That's better.

JEROME: I am reprogramming you. You've taken a layer of skin off my face. You do that again and I'm stripping you down for spares and then dropping you off a twenty-storey building –

NAN: Story-time, now. . .

JEROME: Oh, God . . .

NAN: Once upon a time there were three bears called Jack and Jill who wanted to go to the ball only the other ducklings wouldn't let her play with them . . .

JEROME: Nan, stop.

NAN: Stopped, Nan.

JEROME: Nan, register.

NAN: Register, Nan.

JEROME: (*Standing in front of her so she can scan his face*) Not child. Not child.

NAN: Not child. Registered, Nan.

JEROME: Nan, take a nap.

NAN: Take a nap, Nan.

JEROME: (*Muttering*) I don't know why I bothered to switch you on again, really.
(*She heads back to the bedrooms.*)

NAN: (*Turning suddenly tearful, in her other tone*) I don't know why I bother, Jerome, I really don't. When you treat me like this. I've done everything I possibly can. I can't cope any more. If you want to go and live with her, I don't care. Go on! Go on! Go and live with the bloody woman. See if I care.

9

(*She goes out to the bedrooms.* JEROME *frowns. He sits. The Bach continues to play. After a moment, there is a crash from the bedroom.*)

(*Off*) Oh, for goodness' sake, you extremely stupid old bat. Who put that there, then?

(JEROME *sits once again and closes his eyes, assured of peace at last. After a second, the doorbell rings. The screen lights up once more. It is the video entry-phone system again.* ZOË *is at the front door. She is breathless and dishevelled.*)

ZOË: (*From screen*) Mr Watkins . . .

JEROME: (*Disturbed again*) I don't believe this . . .

ZOË: Mr Watkins! This is Zoë Mill from the Blaise Gillespie Agency. Would you let me in, please?

(*She looks anxiously over her shoulder and rings the doorbell again.* JEROME *crosses to the console. He switches off the music.*)

(*Urgently*) Mr Watkins! Please!

JEROME: (*Pressing the door button at the console*) All right! Push the door.

ZOË: Mr Watkins, open the door . . .

JEROME: Push it. It's open . . .

ZOË: Oh, please say you're in. Please God you're at home . . .
(*She rings the bell again.*)

JEROME: (*Yelling*) It's open. Push the door!

ZOË: I'm going to break it down, Mr Watkins.

(*We see her, on screen, step back and run at the door.* JEROME *presses the door button long and hard.* ZOË *hits the door which opens easily. She disappears. A second later, she appears in the room, a tattered, breathless wreck. She pulls up short, breathing heavily.* JEROME *stares at her incredulously.*)

(*Attempting a semblance of dignity*) Mr Watkins? How do you do? I am sorry to burst in like this. My name is Zoë Mill. From the Blaise Gillespie Agency.

(JEROME *stares at her stupefied.*)

(*After a pause*) I hope they advised you I was coming, I . . .
(*She trails away. On screen, the view of the hallway remains.*)

JEROME: (*Suddenly aware of this*) You've left my front door open . . .

(*He rushes out of the room into the hall, seizing his walking stick as he goes.* ZOË, *alarmed, flinches slightly as he dashes past her.* JEROME *appears briefly on the video screen. We see that his stick is in fact a swordstick which he has now drawn. He checks to left and right, then closes the door. The screen goes blank.* JEROME *returns, sword still drawn.* ZOË *watches him, transfixed.* JEROME *sheathes his sword and replaces the stick near the door.*)
Never leave my front door open.

ZOË: (*Muted*) No. I'm sorry. (*Pause.*) You see, there were these people –

JEROME: I know there are these people. Why the hell do you think I keep it shut?

ZOË: Yes.
(*Another pause.* JEROME *stares at her.* ZOË *tries to pull herself together. It is difficult for her. Her clothes are in ribbons, her face is bleeding from a cut and her hands are torn and filthy. She has lost one shoe and is holding the other. Her stockings are in shreds. She obviously started out looking quite elegant in her smart suit and crisp blouse.*)

JEROME: (*Aware he has been rather rude*) Sorry.

ZOË: No, no. I'm sorry. (*Brightly*) Well, here I am. At last. (*She laughs nervously.*) What a super room.
(JEROME *is staring at her. A pause.*)
(*Nervously indicating a seat*) Is this – for sitting on?

JEROME: (*Guardedly*) Yes.

ZOË: Well. Would you mind if I – ?

JEROME: No.

ZOË: Thanks very much.
(*She sits.* JEROME *continues to stand, staring at her. She gives a sudden, quite unexpected, reflex sob as the shock begins to take hold but elects to continue as if it hadn't happened.*)
I'm sorry if I'm looking a bit of a – I must do a bit. I'm sorry. Anyway, I understood this was just an initial interview. Mrs Hope-Fitch told me you just wanted to look at me. See if I was suitable. But I believe the actual job's not for a week or so? Have I got that right? (*She sobs.*) Excuse me. Yes?

JEROME: (*Thoughtfully*) Yes.

ZOË: (*Indicating herself*) Look, you'll just have to disregard all this. I mean, *this* is ghastly. But I can – you may not believe this – I can look pretty good. Although I say it myself. Yes? But as I say, not – Don't, for God's sake, go by this. (*She sobs.*) Sorry.

(*Silence.*)

Would you like me to – walk up and down? Give you an overall picture? People sometimes find it helps them to – get a more general . . . Of course, I don't know quite what you're looking for so it's a bit . . . I understood it was slightly unusual? Is that so? (*She sobs.*)

JEROME: (*Thoughtfully*) Yes.

ZOË: I'll stand up. (*She does so.*) There.

(JEROME *studies her.*)

Five foot four and a bit. I can lose a bit more weight if you like. I'm a bit over my usual . . . (*She sobs.*) I'll walk about for you. In case you need me to walk. (*She walks about, limping slightly.*) By the way, I don't usually limp, of course. Please, disregard that. I just seemed to have bashed my knee – Anyway. And, naturally, with heels on I'm that bit taller. They help no end, of course, with all sorts of things. God, look at my legs. Don't look at those, either. I'm sorry, I'm afraid you're just going to have to take my word for an awful lot of things. (*She sobs.*) Look, I'm awfully sorry, I think I'm just going to have to go away somewhere and have a quick cry. I'm sorry, I'm just in a bit of a state. I am sorry. Is there a – ? Have you got a – ?

JEROME: Oh yes, yes, sure. There's one just out there. First on the left.

(*He indicates towards the bedrooms.*)

ZOË: I'll be as quick as I can. I'm so sorry.

(ZOË *plunges out of the room. As she reaches the offstage bathroom door, we hear the sudden start of her tears, then the slamming of the door.* JEROME *stares after her, thoughtfully. He goes to his console and winds back a tape. He replays a section.*)

ZOË'S RECORDED VOICE: . . . all sorts of things. God, look at my legs. Don't look at those, either. I'm sorry, I'm afrai – (*Her voice cuts off as* JEROME *stops the tape. He shrugs. He switches the machine back to record. He waits. He fades up a fader on the panel.* ZOË's *sobs are heard over the speaker and the sound of her blowing her nose.*)

ZOË: (*Over the speakers*) Oh, dear God . . .

(JEROME *fades her down and moves away from the console. After a moment,* ZOË *returns with a handful of tissues, wiping her nose.*)

Sorry about that. Here I am. Back again. Anyway, where was I? Yes. Let me tell you about me. I'm originally an actress. Still am, actually. Only I also model to keep the wolf occasionally from the door. And I've been doing this escort thing lately which has been very interesting. Only I understood you didn't just want an escort, you wanted something slightly more. So that's probably why they thought of me. I did have some pictures and my CV to show you as well, only they took my briefcase. (*Getting tearful again*) It wasn't even as if there was anything in there . . . Sorry. There were these terrifying girls, you see . . .

JEROME: Girls?

ZOË: Who attacked me. Just now. On my way here.

JEROME: Attacked you?

ZOË: Girls. Women. I don't know.

JEROME: What did you do to them?

ZOË: (*Rather indignantly*) I didn't do anything. I was just quietly walking here from the station. It was a lovely day and I –

JEROME: *Walked?*

ZOË: Yes.

JEROME: You walked from the railway station to here?

ZOË: Yes. I've just said. And then these monsters . . . came from nowhere. What sort of area is this? Don't you have any police at all? Any security patrols?

JEROME: Not any more.

ZOË: Neighbourhood vigilantes?

JEROME: Not lately.

13

ZOË: You mean, this area is not protected? At all? What about this building?

JEROME: The security staff kept being found dead. It got very expensive . . .

ZOË: My God. Mrs Hope-Fitch might have warned me.

JEROME: What did these people look like?

ZOË: Oh. (*She shudders.*) Awful. No hair at all. Not on their heads, anyway. Masses of it everywhere else. And sort of purple paint across here.

(*She indicates a band across the middle of her face.*)

JEROME: No, that's a tattoo.

ZOË: Really?

JEROME: They're the Daughters of Darkness.

ZOË: Oh. They were female then.

JEROME: Most of them.

ZOË: Well, whatever they were. I didn't stop to introduce myself. I hit the biggest of them and ran as fast as I could . . .

JEROME: (*Stunned*) You hit a Daughter of Darkness?

ZOË: Yes. On the head. With my shoe.

JEROME: Ah.

ZOË: Am I supposed to have done something wrong?

JEROME: Well, I don't think you should have done that.

ZOË: Why not?

JEROME: Well, you may have got them angry.

ZOË: Angry? What about my briefcase . . .

JEROME: Was there anything important in your briefcase?

ZOË: No, I've just said, just my –

JEROME: Then it would have been simpler to have given it to them.

ZOË: But I don't see why I should have just handed it over. It was a present from my ex-boyfriend.

JEROME: You may have made things difficult.

ZOË: (*Sarcastically*) Well, oh dear, oh dear. That's all I can say.

JEROME: For you.

ZOË: How do you mean?

JEROME: Well. When you want to get back, they may not let you back . . .

14

ZOË: You mean . . . ? But . . . ? How do I . . . ? I can't stay here indefinitely, can I?

JEROME: No, no . . .

ZOË: If they won't let me out, then we'd better call the police, hadn't we? Or whatever it is that passes for the law round here . . .

JEROME: I'm afraid that's them. They pass for the law round here. They are the law.

ZOË: The Daughters of –

JEROME: Darkness. Yes. Currently.

ZOË: Well, in that case, I'm sorry. I had no idea I was hitting a policeman, I can assure you. Where I come from they don't have purple stripes tattooed across their faces. You mean this is a genuine no-go area? My God, I've only read about them till now. Mind you, I've never been this far up the Northern Line before. Where are we? Somewhere extraordinary. Edgware. I went to Balham once but that's the other way, isn't it? How absolutely terrifying. So what happens now?

JEROME: It's all right. I'll talk to them. I have a relationship with them. Of sorts. I do things for them, now and then.

ZOË: Do what?

JEROME: I help rig their sound gear when they have their big concerts. Things like that.

ZOË: Oh, how interesting. Are you a roadie?

JEROME: Not really. It's just a hobby.

ZOË: What is it you do?

JEROME: I'm a composer.

ZOË: How amazing. Well. Hence – (*she indicates the sound console*) – hence all that.

(*A sudden violent clang from one of the windows.* ZOË *is startled.*)

What on earth is that?

JEROME: That's the Daughters.

ZOË: What are they doing?

JEROME: Throwing bricks at the window shutters. They're showing their displeasure.

(*Another clang.* ZOË *winces.*)

15

It's all right, they're half-inch steel. They'll probably keep this up for an hour or two. Till they think of something else to do.

(*Another clang.*)

ZOË: Lucky you had your shutters closed.

JEROME: Hardly lucky. They're welded to the window frames. They haven't been opened in four years.

(*Another clang. She winces.*)

ZOË: They can't get in, can they?

JEROME: Not unless they can jump thirty feet. It's all right.

(*Another clang. A silence.*)

I think they've gone.

(*They listen again.*)

Yes.

(*She relaxes slightly. A pause.*)

It's quieter where you live, then?

ZOË: Yes, we're – pretty lucky in Kilburn. Regular armed patrols, masses of security cameras and so on. Very well lit, most of it. I mean, actually, the High Street's brighter at night than it is in the daytime. Providing you're in by dusk you're fine. I've had no trouble. Not really. Couple of burglaries, that's all. Oh, and my dog was shot, that was sad, but we think that was an accident. We think someone must have mistaken him for a police dog.

JEROME: Shame. We?

ZOË: My ex-boyfriend.

JEROME: Ah.

ZOË: He's still living with me but he's definitely my ex-boyfriend. Still. Enough about me. To business.

JEROME: Yes.

ZOË: You must tell me about this job you'd like me to do. Assuming you'd like me to do it, of course?

JEROME: Yes.

ZOË: You're still deciding?

JEROME: Yes.

ZOË: Oh, right. Sorry. Do you want me to walk up and down again?

JEROME: No.

16

ZOE: (*Laughing*) I could do you a bit of Shakespeare. Any good?
No.

JEROME: I wonder if you'd mind – trying on some clothes.

ZOE: (*Suspiciously*) What sort of clothes?

JEROME: Just normal clothes. Women's clothing.

ZOE: I'm the one trying them on?

JEROME: Yes.

ZOE: Where? I mean, where do you want me to try them on?

JEROME: Here.

ZOE: You mean in front of you?

JEROME: Yes.

ZOE: You want me to change my clothes in front of you, is that
it?

JEROME: No. I want you to change into different clothes
elsewhere. And then come in here so I can look at you
wearing those different clothes in front of me. That I'll give
you. To wear. You.

ZOE: (*Considering this proposition*) Yes, that sounds OK. I'm
sorry. It's just occasionally, you know, we get – sort of
weird requests, you know. The old favourites, you know.
Nuns and gymslips.

JEROME: Oh, no.

ZOE: Fine.

JEROME: Nothing like that.

ZOE: No, sorry. Just thought I'd . . .

JEROME: These are my wife's clothes.
(*A silence.*)

ZOE: Your wife's?

JEROME: Yes. They're quite ordinary clothes. They may be a
bit out of fashion but –

ZOE: Your wife, is she – ?

JEROME: What?

ZOE: Is she dead at all?

JEROME: Dead?

ZOE: Yes.

JEROME: No, she's –

ZOE: She's still alive?

JEROME: Yes.

17

ZOË: Living with you?

JEROME: No. We're separated.

ZOË: Oh. (*She breathes more easily.*) I'm sorry.

JEROME: If you don't mind my saying so, you seem rather wary.

ZOË: Well. Yes. I'm sorry. Look, this is my first time. As an escort. And I was assured that there was nothing further entailed, other than escorting. But then I get here and find you on your own, asking me to try on clothes. I got panicked. Sorry. I'm a little bit shaky still, I – Give me the clothes. I'll put them on for you. No more questions. (*Slapping her own face*) Zoë, grow up and be your age.

JEROME: Wait there.

(*He goes out to the bedrooms.* ZOË *looks about her.*)

ZOË: (*To herself*) Nevertheless. This is a very, very creepy set-up. It has to be said.

(*She wanders about looking at the room for the first time, intrigued by the console. She is examining this when the doorbell rings and the nightmarish face of one of the Daughters of Darkness appears on the screen, leering into the video camera.*)

Oh, dear God, it's them . . . (*She hurries towards the bedroom doorway.*) Mr Watkins . . . Mr Watkins . . . I think it's them. They're at the door –

(JEROME *hurriedly returns with a long dress, similar to the one that* NAN *was wearing, a blouse and a pair of shoes. The face remains on the screen murmuring inaudible obscenities.*)

(*Indicating the screen*) There! That's one of them.

JEROME: Oh, she's OK. That's Rita. She's our local representative. She's fairly friendly. I'll have a word with her. (*Handing her the clothes*) Try these. The dress should be all right. I don't know about the shoes. We can always buy some others.

ZOË: Don't let her in here.

JEROME: Certainly not. She's not that friendly.

(*She takes the bundle. He picks up his swordstick and goes out. After a second he appears on the screen and we see him and the Daughter of Darkness engaged in an inaudible, urgent-looking*

18

conversation. ZOË, *rather nervous now she's alone, glances at the screen, notes* JEROME *is busy and decides to change where she is. She undresses to her slip. There is a small sound from the direction of the bedrooms.* ZOË *starts, glances at the screen and, hearing nothing more and seeing* JEROME, *relaxes again. She sits and taking up the clean blouse is fiddling with one of the fastenings on it, prior to putting it on, when* NAN *appears in the bedroom doorway.* ZOË *does not see her.* NAN *watches her for a moment, then produces her face flannel.*)

NAN: (*Playfully*) Booo! Nan's coming to getcher!
(ZOË *turns, sees her, but is too late to dodge. She screams.* NAN *sets about* ZOË's *face with her flannel.* ZOË *screams and struggles but her cries are mostly muffled. Unnoticed,* JEROME *finishes his on-screen conversation. In due course, he closes the front door on Rita and the screen blanks again.*)

ZOË: (*Spluttering*) Hot hoo hooing hoo hee? Het ho! Hoff! Het Hoff!

NAN: That's better. That's better. There's a nice clean face.
(*As she says this,* NAN *goes off at speed to the kitchen.*)

ZOË: (*Calling after her, indignantly*) What were you doing? What did you think you were doing? Oh, dear God.
(*She grabs up the clothes and prepares to flee towards the front door. She all but runs into* JEROME.)
There's a – There was a –

JEROME: Anything wrong?

ZOË: A woman just came in and washed my face –

JEROME: Oh, yes.

ZOË: What do you mean, 'oh, yes'? Who is she? What was she doing?

JEROME: It's all right, she registered you as a child, you see. That's all.
(*A crash from the kitchen.*)
Unless she's told otherwise she registers everyone as children.

ZOË: Who is she? Is that your wife?

JEROME: No, no. She's a NAN 300F. She's a machine. She's just a machine.

19

ZOË: *That* – was a machine? I don't believe it.

JEROME: Oh, yes.

ZOË: Well, what is it? Where did it come from?

JEROME: It – er – it came from the man just down the hall, actually.

ZOË: The man down the hall?

JEROME: Yes.

ZOË: I'm going. All right? I'll borrow these clothes. I promise to post them back. I'm sorry, I don't think this job is for me after all. I think I'll just stick around a little longer and hope for a fringe revival of *Hedda Gabler*. (*She makes to go into the hall*.)

JEROME: Are you thinking of leaving?

ZOË: I most certainly am. I'm not stopping here with that – deranged machine, thank you very much.

JEROME: I – wouldn't go just yet –

ZOË: Why?

JEROME: Well, I don't think the Daughters would be too happy if you tried to leave. Not until your case comes up before Council.

ZOË: Council?

JEROME: They're considering it at the next Council.

ZOË: When's that?

JEROME: Midnight.

ZOË: Midnight? I'm not sitting here till midnight . . . I mean, they can't . . . I've got masses of . . . They can just – they can simply go and –
(*A single loud clang on the shutters*.)
(*Facing the inevitable*) What happens at midnight, then?

JEROME: They'll consider your case.

ZOË: Do I have to be there?

JEROME: Not unless you want to be.

ZOË: No, thanks very much. What'll happen?

JEROME: Rita thinks you'll get away with a fine. It would have been worse but – I put in a word.

ZOË: (*Sarcastically*) Lucky I met you, really.

JEROME: Do you have money with you?

ZOË: I'm not a complete idiot . . . I have credit cards on me.

20

JEROME: (*Curious*) Where?

ZOË: Never you mind. Will they do?

JEROME: Possibly. I know they take cheques. Listen, do you want to –
(*He indicates her state of undress.*)

ZOË: Oh, yes. Since I appear to be here for the night, I'd better get dressed, I suppose.

JEROME: There's a bedroom along there if you –

ZOË: Where is the thing?

JEROME: In the kitchen. It's all right, I'll keep her away.

ZOË: Please do. (*She moves to the doorway.*) There aren't any more of them, are there?

JEROME: No. Second door on the right.

ZOË: Won't be long.
(*She goes off to the bedrooms.* JEROME *frowns, as he is still undecided about her. He crosses to the console and fades up a fader.*)
(*Through the speakers, muttering*) . . . trapped in this place till midnight with a raving lunatic and a homicidal tin woman is hardly my idea of a good time . . .
(JEROME *fades her down. He stops a tape machine and rewinds it a little. He replays a section. The voices come over the speakers.*)

ZOË'S RECORDED VOICE: (*Spluttering*) Hot hoo hooing hoo hee? Het ho! Hoff! Het Hoff!

MAN'S RECORDED VOICE: That's better. That's better. There's a nice clean face.

ZOË'S RECORDED VOICE: (*Indignantly*) What were you doing? What did you think you were doing? Oh, dear God.
(JEROME *stops the tape and rewinds a fraction. He replays again.*)
What were you doing? What did you think – (*He rewinds.*) What were you doing? (*He stops the tape.*)

JEROME: No. (*He shakes his head.*) No, no, no.
(*He hears* ZOË *returning. He hastily switches on the recorder again and moves away from the console.* ZOË *enters. She has on the dress, blouse and shoes.*)

ZOË: The clothes are fine. The shoes are a fraction large but –

What do you think?

(*She poses to allow him to inspect her.* JEROME *studies her from several angles.*)

JEROME: Does your hair – Does it come down at all?

ZOË: Oh, yes. Do you want me to – ?

JEROME: Would you mind?

ZOË: No. (*She takes the clips from her hair.*) I don't usually wear it down because it makes me look about ten. But – if that's what you're looking for . . . There! Is that more the thing?

JEROME: (*Impressed*) It's – it's excellent.

ZOË: Oh. Good. Well. Good.

JEROME: Excellent.

ZOË: You still haven't really said –

JEROME: Would you mind laughing for me?

ZOË: Laughing?

JEROME: Is that possible?

ZOË: Yes. Hang on. That's one of the things I'm never very good at. I can cry very well. Floods of tears at the drop of a hat. No? OK. (*She tries*) Ha! Ha!

(JEROME *looks dubious.*)

Sorry, that was awful. I can do miles better than that. Ha! Ha! No. Think of something funny, Zoë. Ha! Ha! You don't happen to know any jokes, do you? No, I didn't think you did. Ho! Ho! Ho! God, this is awful. Thank heavens my drama teacher isn't here. Haw! Haw! Haw! (*As her laughs get progressively worse*) Look, could we leave it for a second and come back to it. I could do you my piece of Shakespeare . . .

JEROME: No, that's quite all right. Don't worry at all. I realize it must be very –

ZOË: Well, it is very difficult if you haven't any real – motivation, you see.

JEROME: Oh, yes.

ZOË: I mean, frankly, not an awful lot's happened to me recently that makes me want to scream with laughter.

JEROME: Please don't worry at all.

ZOË: So, you want me to walk about with my hair down, laughing in a long dress . . . Any other requirements? I mean, what's it all for? Are we selling something?

JEROME: Please. Sit down.

ZOË: Thank you.

(*She sits.*)

JEROME: Just a moment.

(*He moves to the console again, this time looking for a video recording from the cupboards.* ZOË *waits patiently.* NAN *enters from the kitchen. She carries a drinking glass and a plate, both of which are upside down.* ZOË, *frozen, watches* NAN.)

ZOË: (*In a whisper*) Mr Watkins . . . Mr Watkins . . .

JEROME: (*From the cupboard*) Hallo?

ZOË: It's – it's back again.

NAN: (*Putting the things down and turning to* ZOË) There we are, doesn't that look lovely? Doesn't that look good?

ZOË: (*Nervously*) Oh, yes. Lovely, lovely . . .

(NAN *moves swiftly to her, producing a coloured bow from her pocket which she fastens in the protesting* ZOË'S *hair.*)

(*As* NAN *does this*) Ah, now – don't you – don't you start that – Mr Watkins . . .

NAN: There! There! There!

JEROME: (*Seeing what's happening*) Oh, yes. Sorry – it's all right, you're perfectly safe . . . Nan, stop.

NAN: Stopped, Nan.

(NAN *freezes by* ZOË, *who escapes, looking slightly ludicrous with her hair now in a top-knot.*)

JEROME: She's still registering you as a child, that's all. We'll re-register you, then she won't bother you.

ZOË: Anything. I mean, I know my hair like this makes me look younger but this is ridiculous . . .

JEROME: Could you just stand facing her, so she can scan you.

(ZOË *stands some distance away.*)

ZOË: Like this?

JEROME: A bit closer. Would you mind?

ZOË: (*Moving closer*) I don't like the way it's looking at me.

JEROME: That's just your imagination. She's not thinking of anything. She's actually on standby.

ZOË: Yes, I think I've acted with one or two people like this.

JEROME: Nan, register.

23

NAN: Register, Nan.

JEROME: Not child. Not child.

NAN: Not child. Registered, Nan.

JEROME: There we are.

ZOË: (*Stepping away*) Is that it?

JEROME: Yes. She's now recorded you as an adult – well, rather as a non-child – so she shouldn't bother you at all now.

ZOË: (*Removing the hair bow gingerly*) Was it designed to look after children?

JEROME: Yes. Well, technically, narrower than that. To look after a child. It was felt that the programming got too complex to deal with several children. So it was designed to deal with just one individual. Then that was it. It shut down automatically and you had to give it a whole new factory programme. It was a safety measure to prevent one being reused, you see. On a mismatched child. Well, so this man was telling me –

ZOË: This would be the man down the hall –

JEROME: That's right.

ZOË: Why did he give it to you?

JEROME: Ah, well. He was a designer for the firm that made them. But they went bankrupt and he moved away. He really only left me this for spares. I got her working again myself. Just for my own amusement, really.

ZOË: But how can it still work? I mean, I thought you said they shut down once they . . . ?

JEROME: Yes, they do. I don't think this one's ever been matched to a child, though. She's a prototype.

ZOË: You mean that's why she thought I was . . .

JEROME: Yes. She lives in hope. Don't you, Nan?

(NAN *reactivates at the sound of her name.*)

NAN: I'll do the beds now. Time to do the beds.

(NAN *goes off towards the bedrooms.*)

JEROME: Random programming. If you don't tell her what to do, after a time she just selects something from her memory.

ZOË: Seems quite sad, in a way. Wandering about, looking for a child to look after. Unfulfilled, almost. In so far as a machine can be unfulfilled, of course. I suppose no more so than, say, a coffee grinder that can't find any beans to grind could be described as unfulfilled.

JEROME: Well, there's more to her than a coffee grinder.

ZOË: Oh, yes. But one mustn't empathize with machines, must one? They say that's fatal. Mind you, I do that all the time. I shout and scream at my washing machine. (*She laughs.*) There! That was quite a good laugh, wasn't it? Why did they go bankrupt? The firm that made them? I'd have thought they'd have sold like hot cakes. What happened?

JEROME: Er . . . They were very expensive. And – (*he seems evasive*) – there were teething problems.

ZOË: (*Suspiciously*) Were there?

JEROME: (*Reflectively*) I think the biggest mistake they made was to make a machine so sophisticated and then give it too small a function. I mean, I think a machine that complex needed more than just a child to look after. Otherwise there's bound to be stress.

ZOË: Possibly. Yes. What an interesting theory. You mean, a machine with a certain sized brain can actually have too little to do?

JEROME: Too little to think about.

ZOË: Yes. Quite a theory.

JEROME: That's why I tried for a time to –

ZOË: To what?

JEROME: Give her some other thoughts. Feed in other memories. Particularly with her having no child, I thought it might . . .

ZOË: Did it help?

JEROME: I don't know that it did, really. Still. It was worth a try.
(*A silence. He seems steeped in thought again.* ZOË *studies him.*)

ZOË: Did you say you were a composer?

JEROME: Right.

ZOË: What sort of music do you compose?

JEROME: All sorts.

ZOË: I mean, is it – you know – popular sort of music?

25

JEROME: Not very, no.

ZOË: No, you know what I mean – as opposed to classical music?

JEROME: I don't write classical music, either. I'd need to have been dead several hundred years . . .

ZOË: Well, what do you write?

JEROME: I write – modern music.

ZOË: Would I know it? I mean, would I have heard any? Only it would be nice to tell people when I get home – that's if I get home – I met *the* Mr Watkins.

JEROME: Jerome.

ZOË: Jerome, right. *The* Jerome. Do call me Zoë.

JEROME: Tell your friends that if they remember those baby-powder commercials they showed two or three years ago, ten times a night, every night for about eight months – then you met the man who wrote that music and wished to God he hadn't.

ZOË: What you mean the – the one with the singing babies?
(JEROME *nods wearily*.)
(*Excitedly*) All those sweet little singing babies? But that was absolutely brilliant. Did you do the music for that? But that was absolutely fantastic. That was wonderful. That was so clever. That was completely and utterly *brilliant*. You're an absolute genius.

JEROME: Thank you.

ZOË: Oh, I wish they'd bring that back. It was so good. Brilliant. Gosh. I'm very impressed. What else have you written?

JEROME: About three hundred other pieces.

ZOË: Any more with singing babies?

JEROME: No, no. No more singing babies.

ZOË: What else?

JEROME: (*Wearily*) Three string quartets. An unaccompanied cello sonata. Several pieces for synthesizer . . .

ZOË: No, I don't know any of those. Tell me, I bet everybody asks you this – how did you get all those babies singing in tune?
(JEROME *looks at her incredulously*.)

26

Or is that a closely guarded secret?

JEROME: Yes. I'm afraid it's very – closely guarded.

ZOË: (*Disappointed*) Oh. Brilliant, anyway.

JEROME: (*Without malice*) Would you describe yourself as an intelligent person?

ZOË: Me?

JEROME: Yes.

ZOË: Heavens! I don't know. As an actress friend of mine used to say – it depends on the script, dear.
(*She laughs.*)

JEROME: (*Nodding*) Yes. That's a good point. That's a very good point.

ZOË: It's an intellectual role this then, is it?

JEROME: No. Just reasonably intelligent. I was just wondering –

ZOË: Oh, I can come over as pretty clever, you know. I did Arkadina in *The Seagull* – do you know it?

JEROME: No.

ZOË: Chekhov. I mean she's often played as quite stupid but I don't think she is. Of course, I was much too young for her . . . (*Pause*) Shall I walk around again for you?

JEROME: No.
(ZOË *restlessly walks about.*)

ZOË: And I played the wife in *See How They Run*. She's no fool, either. (*Pause. At the console, pretending to play a keyboard*) Diddly-diddly diddly dom. Is this where you compose?

JEROME: Uh-huh.

ZOË: Brilliant. What is it?

JEROME: It's a digital audio system.

ZOË: Ah-ha!

JEROME: Which I use primarily for sampling and synthesizing aural sounds.

ZOË: Brilliant. Whey-hey. Diddly-diddly –

JEROME: Please don't touch anything. Please.

ZOË: No, no. Sorry. I promise.
(NAN *comes through busily with a bundle of dirty sheets* en route *to the kitchen, humming to herself.*)

27

What on earth is it doing?

JEROME: Oh, she'll do that for hours. It keeps her happy.

ZOË: Oh. (*Slight pause.*) Are you still deciding?

JEROME: Yes.

ZOË: OK. Don't mind me. I can't go anywhere, anyway. (*She studies the console; reading*) What do 'bedroom one', 'bedroom two' and 'bathroom' mean?

JEROME: Just an experiment.

ZOË: Something you were composing?

JEROME: That's right.

ZOË: A bathroom suite.
   (*She laughs.*)

JEROME: (*Meaning her laugh*) Very good, very good.

ZOË: Pretty good for me. (*She laughs again.*) I very rarely make jokes.

JEROME: Jokes?

ZOË: Just then. I made a joke. Didn't you – ? Oh, you meant the laugh? You liked the laugh?

JEROME: Very good. Excellent.
   (*He has risen.*)

ZOË: Thank you. I'll put that on my CV. (*Scowling*) When I get some more done. Special skills include laughing.

JEROME: Let me show you something . . .
   (JEROME *goes to the console and starts the video recording he has located earlier. In a moment, the screen lights up. A young girl of about nine appears on the screen. Conventionally pretty, fair-haired and slightly self-conscious.*)

YOUNG GEAIN: Hallo, Daddy. This is Geain. I'm just calling to say thank you very much for all my presents. They were all really live. Especially the disc voucher which I'm going to spend on the new Jamie Butterscotch and one by The Grind. Mummy gave me a long dress which is really live. It's yellow and grey and Granny and Grandpa gave me some live jewellery to go with it and I'm going to wear that tonight because we're going out to dinner to Del – to Del something – I can't remember. I wish you were coming, Daddy. And I miss you very much. And I hope to see you soon. Bye. Love from Geain. (*She makes a big cross in the*

28

air with her finger.) That's a kiss.
(JEROME *stops the tape and looks at* ZOË *who realizes she is supposed to comment.*)

ZOË: That's your daughter?

JEROME: Yes.

ZOË: Lovely.

JEROME: Thank you.
(*Slight pause.*)

ZOË: I couldn't play her.

JEROME: Oh, no . . .

ZOË: You don't want that?

JEROME: No.

ZOË: Oh, good. (*Pause.*) How old is she?

JEROME: Geain? She'll be thirteen.

ZOË: Thirteen? She looks quite young for her age.

JEROME: Oh, that was recorded – some time ago.

ZOË: I see.

JEROME: That was probably the last occasion I was permitted to see her.

ZOË: Really?

JEROME: Her mother – my wife wouldn't let her phone me after that. She wouldn't let me visit her. She wouldn't let Geain visit me.

ZOË: Who not?

JEROME: Why not? Because my wife is a selfish, vindictive, unforgiving bitch.

ZOË: Oh, I see. Yes. (*A pause.*) Do you want me to play her, then?

JEROME: (*Angrily*) No, I don't want you to play her.

ZOË: No, right. Sorry, sorry.
(NAN *comes through again with the same bundle of sheets, bound for the bedroom once more.*)
I think I'd better go and give her a hand in a minute.
(*She laughs feebly.* JEROME *is silent again.*)
It's a nice name, Jane. *Jane Eyre.* We did that one. I played the mad Mrs Rochester. Behind the panelling. Not much of a part. I should have played Jane, really. I'd have been really good.

29

JEROME: G–E–A–I–N.

ZOË: Sorry?

JEROME: Ours is spelt G–E–A–I–N. At her mother's insistence.

ZOË: How unusual. What is it? Gaelic?

JEROME: No, just pretentious.

ZOË: I'd love to have children of my own. Well, for about twenty minutes, anyway. Sometimes I think, wouldn't it be lovely to hear them rushing about the flat, laughing and yelling? And then – at about six in the morning I think, no, it wouldn't at all, I can't think of anything worse. But I suppose with the right man – someone who'd share them – do all the cleaning up – possibly they'd be everything I ever wanted. But I doubt it. I suppose you're either maternal or you aren't. I know which I am.

JEROME: (*Who has been staring at her, coming to a sudden decision*) All right. We'll give it a try. The proposition is this. I want you to live here with me for twenty-four hours as my loving, caring companion –

ZOË: Ah, now, listen, I thought we'd been through all that –

JEROME: In just about a week's time, my wife and my daughter, together with some – petty official from the Social Services – are coming here, to this flat, for the first time in four years. And between them, my wife and this official will decide whether or not they consider this a fit place and, more important, whether they consider me a fit person for her to spend time with in the future. On their one visit everything rests. If I fail to meet their high standards of homeliness and hygiene, then it's unlikely I shall be allowed to see my daughter again.

ZOË: Unless you visit her.

JEROME: Visit her? Where?

ZOË: Where she lives.

JEROME: She lives with my wife. How can I visit there? The woman loathes the sight of me.

ZOË: She's coming here, though.

JEROME: She's coming here to make damn sure she prevents any future visit by Geain. I've told you, Corinna is a very vindictive, unforgiving woman.

30

ZOË: Unforgiving of what?

JEROME: (*Evasively*) Unforgiving of – anything you care to mention.

ZOË: So you need to present them with a solid domestic front.

JEROME: I want to present them with a relationship that's so perfect that not only can she not find fault with it, but it doubles her up with jealousy. It leaves her eating her heart out with envy and frustration.

ZOË: Yes. (*Tentatively*) If you don't mind my saying so – it's beginning to sound a wee bit vindictive on both sides –

JEROME: How do you mean?

ZOË: Well –

JEROME: I have cause. I have cause to be vindictive –

ZOË: Oh, yes. Only –

JEROME: (*Excitedly*) She's not the one who's been forbidden to see her own daughter. Denied all those precious moments watching her child grow up. She's not the one who's been left to live alone in an empty flat. Unable to work – unable to write a single note of music for four years. Four years!

ZOË: (*Alarmed*) Yes.

JEROME: Nothing.

ZOË: No.

JEROME: And you talk about me being vindictive. (*Turning on her, angrily*) Who's side are you on? You're taking her side and you haven't even met her . . .

ZOË: No, I'm not. Honestly, I'm not –

JEROME: Do you want this job or don't you?

ZOË: Yes, yes . . .

JEROME: Because if you don't, I can quite easily . . .

ZOË: No, I do. I want it very much. I do honestly. Please, please, please!

(*A silence.* JEROME *simmers down.*)

JEROME: (*Muttering*) God, you bloody women. You don't half stick together, don't you?

ZOË: Not really.

JEROME: My sister, right or wrong. Yes?

ZOË: Not at all. Don't be –

JEROME: What? Don't be what?

31

ZOË: (*Changing tack*) I think I could be the perfect female companion. For twenty-four hours, anyway. I think I could do that. Not much longer though. Mind you, my ex-boyfriend would claim I couldn't even manage it for twenty-four hours. (*Expansively*) Hallo! Welcome! Welcome! Welcome!

JEROME: (*Anxiously*) Yes, I don't want anything too . . .

ZOË: No, well, I'll work on it. Do you think I should wear glasses? Do you think it's a glasses part?

JEROME: No, I don't.

ZOË: No. Still, I need something. I always need some little thing to start off with. Some actors always start with the shoes. (*Gazing at her feet*) I don't think I'll start with these, somehow. I can do quite a deep voice. Shall I give her a deep voice? Like this?

JEROME: (*Alarmed by her enthusiasm*) No, no, please. Just your normal voice. Just be your normal self. Please.

ZOË: (*Calming down*) OK. I could do the limp like that thing out there . . . (*She mimics* NAN's *walk*.) No, only joking. Well, OK. I accept.

JEROME: Good.

ZOË: Actually, it's quite handy me being stuck here. I mean, it gives me a chance to research, you know. Talk to you. Find out what constitutes your perfect mate.

JEROME: So long as we convince them.

ZOË: Oh, yes. Only it helps if I don't pour you a large Scotch when you're a teetotaller. Those sort of things tend to give the game away. (*Pause.*) Or cooking you chicken when you're a vegetarian. (*Finding the burnt tinfoil dish*) Or baking home-made cakes when you're on a diet . . . Is this one of those new self-cooking dishes?

JEROME: That's right.

ZOË: How was it?

JEROME: Delicious.

ZOË: (*Doubtfully examining the burnt dish*) Yes. (*Pause.*) Talking of food and drink. Would it sound awful – ? Only I did start out very early this morning. And my ex-boyfriend had polished off the muesli.

JEROME: Oh yes, certainly, I'll see what we have. I've just stocked up, there's quite a bit of frozen stuff.

ZOË: No, I'll do it. Don't bother.

JEROME: That's OK, I'll . . .

ZOË: No, no, please. Let me. Start getting into the role. Little woman in kitchen. (*She starts for the kitchen, then stops.*) Where's the thing?

JEROME: In the bedroom.

ZOË: OK. Watch this then. A startling character transformation.

(ZOË *marches out to the kitchen while* JEROME *watches rather apprehensively. She comes straight back again.*)

I'm sorry, I'm not going in there. My God, what have you been doing?

JEROME: What?

ZOË: It's *disgusting* out there. It's *revolting*. It's swimming in – yuurrrk. Uggh! Ugghh! It's your ghastly machine. It must be.

JEROME: She does – spill things.

ZOË: Spill things? She's tipped whole piles of festering food all over everything. You should be dead, you know. It's a miracle you're alive . . . I tell you, that machine is a –

JEROME: All right, I'll do it.

ZOË: I'm not eating *anything* from there –

JEROME: It's instant stuff. It's sealed. I'll just put it in the oven.

ZOË: Well, make sure we open it in here . . .

JEROME: Whatever you say.

(*He goes out to the kitchen.* ZOË, *left alone, decides to practise her role. She takes up the stance of a beaming hostess.*)

ZOË: (*Brightly*) Hallo! Hallo! Hallo! Welcome! Welcome! Welcome! Sorry. I completely lost track of the time. Typical. (*Turning as if hearing someone calling*) What's that? Just a tick, darling. I'm coming, darling.

(*As she is doing this,* NAN *comes from the bedrooms. She has finally got rid of the sheets. She is heading towards the hall. But she sees* ZOË *and stops, staring at her impassively.*)

(*Seeing* NAN) Oh, hallo, I was just . . .

(NAN *moves off to the hall and goes out.*)

33

Mind your own business, anyway.

(*She is about to start again when the phone rings.*)

JEROME: (*Off*) Leave that. It'll go on to answer.

(ZOË *waits.* LUPUS *appears on the screen after the phone has rung a couple of times. He is seated at a drum kit which he has set up around his video machine. We can see part of this. He is slightly more wild-eyed than before and possibly suffering from the effects of some stimulant.* ZOË *stares at him incredulously.*)

LUPUS: (*From the video*) Hiya, Jerry. I seem to have got the old answering machine again – but on the offchance you're there and would like to register as the only person left in the world who is still prepared to talk to me, here I am. Calling on my final life raft, my only friend, my single ray of hope in the dark endless tunnel some of us laughingly refer to as life. I'm afraid it's down to you, Jerry. You stand between one man and the end of his tether. His final straw. His last burning bridge.

(*Under this,* JEROME *returns from the kitchen with two packets.*)

JEROME: Do you want Breast of Grouse en Croûte or Gourmet Chicken with Almonds and Wild Strawberry Sauce?

ZOË: (*Not inspired by either*) Grouse.

JEROME: There is Sliced Beef in Clam Sauce.

ZOË: Grouse.

JEROME: OK. I think I'll try this chicken.

ZOË: There's an extraordinary man on your phone in a desperate state.

JEROME: Yes, I know. It takes twenty seconds. Can you wait?

(JEROME *goes off to the kitchen.* LUPUS *has been going under this.*)

LUPUS: You may have gathered that my wife has gone. My son has gone. Our furniture has gone. Everything. But for the last time, Jerry. Whoever she's with this time, she can stay with him. I'm not letting her back in. Not this time. She chose to leave, by the way, whilst I went for a job which incidentally I never got. The dynamic geriatric Finchley tea-dance trio decided they could manage without me. Their Arts Council grant came through and they celebrated

34

by buying a drum machine. (*He laughs heartily and mirthlessly.*) So, here we are, sitting amongst this load of obsolete gear (*Smashes a cymbal*) – that nobody wants – (*Hits a drum*) – why hear the real thing when you can hear a synthesized mock-up – (*Another whack of a cymbal*) – I thought you might like to hear it, Jerry, before I burn it all – the last live drum solo, as played by man. The very last. (JEROME *returns. He holds a cloth round the two now very hot tinfoil dishes.* ZOË, *who has been watching the screen transfixed, springs up.* LUPUS *is preparing himself to start a drum solo.*)

JEROME: Look out, they're hot.

ZOË: Sorry, I'll – clear some space . . . There's this extraordinary man. Is he all right?

JEROME: (*Dismissively*) Yes, he's fine. He's always like that.
(LUPUS *starts to play the drums.*)
Oh, for God's sake. Lupus!
(JEROME *dives for the console and turns down the volume.* LUPUS *thrashes away silently for some minutes under the next.*)
Hang on. I'll get some cutlery.
(ZOË *gives him a look.*)
I'll wash it first, don't worry.
(JEROME *goes out.* NAN *has entered, holding the nozzle of a vacuum cleaner but unattached to any machine. She stops behind* ZOË.)

ZOË: (*Calling to* JEROME) I think I'd feel happier if you could boil everything before I touch it, please.

NAN: (*Quietly and venomously*) Making ourselves comfortable, are we, Deborah?

ZOË: (*Jumping round in alarm*) What?

NAN: I know what you're after, dear, and you're not going to have him. If you want Jerome, the only way you're going to get him is over my dead body, you calculating little trollop.

ZOË: (*Very indignant*) I beg your pardon.

NAN: You'd better watch your step, Deborah darling, or one of these nights you're going to wake up with your throat cut.
(NAN *moves away and goes off to the bedrooms.* ZOË *stares at her in horror. She clutches her throat.* JEROME *returns with some knives and forks and two tins of beer.*)

35

JEROME: Here.

ZOË: (*Recoiling*) Ah!

JEROME: You OK?

ZOË: Yes – it was – hot.

JEROME: Good. I brought some beer. I thought you'd prefer the can rather than our glasses. (*He opens both the meals.*) That's yours. I think.

ZOË: Thank you.

JEROME: (*Examining his own dish*) Yes, I think these must be the wild strawberries. Do you want beer?

ZOË: Please.

(JEROME *opens the beers.*)

JEROME: Go ahead, do start. Before it gets rusty. (*She tries it.*)

ZOË: Mmm! Not bad.

JEROME: Hot enough?

ZOË: Perfect.

(*They eat.*)

How long were you married? To Corinna?

JEROME: Eleven years.

ZOË: God. A lifetime. Must have felt very strange. Splitting up.

JEROME: Yes.

ZOË: I mean, even if you loathed the sight of each other.

JEROME: Yes.

ZOË: Was she a musician?

JEROME: Corinna? (*He laughs.*) No. She was my bank manager. Until I moved my account.

ZOË: Do you miss her?

JEROME: No.

ZOË: Would you ever consider going back to her?

JEROME: Look, what the hell is this? A census?

ZOË: I just want to know. I need to know.

JEROME: Why? Why do you want to know all that?

ZOË: Because I'll need to. If I'm to behave like someone who's been living with you for some time, I'll need to know.

JEROME: Well, you don't need to know all that. I'll tell you what you need to know, don't worry.

ZOË: OK. Fine. Fire ahead.

36

(*A pause.*)

JEROME: (*Grumpily*) What do you want to know?

ZOË: No, no. I'm not asking any more questions. You tell me.

JEROME: It's all right . . .

ZOË: No, if I ask questions you just bite my head off. You can tell me, go on.

JEROME: I'm sorry. I – I haven't really talked to anyone – well, not face to face – for some time, you see. Since they fully automated the hypermarket, I don't think I've spoken to anyone for months. So, you'll have to make allowances.

ZOË: I understand.

JEROME: So. If you want to ask questions. Please.

ZOË: Right.

(*They eat.*)

JEROME: Go ahead.

ZOË: I will. I'm just trying to think of some. Why did your wife leave you?

JEROME: I don't think that's any of your damn business.

ZOË: Oh, terrific . . . Forget it. I'll just make it up. I'll make it all up. Just don't blame me if it all goes totally wrong. When it turns out that I don't know vital facts about you that I should know –

JEROME: I just don't see that you need to –

ZOË: Look. If it transpires that your wife left you because for eleven years – or whatever it was – you drove her absolutely mad whistling in the nude at breakfast time – then that's something I ought to know. Because it just might crop up in conversation between the two of us. 'Darling, doesn't he drive you mad the way he whistles in the nude at breakfast?' 'No, not at all, dear, I love it, I find it totally refreshing . . .'

JEROME: All right, all right. My wife left me because . . . She claimed I drove her mad –

ZOË: Whistling in the nude at breakfast – ? Sorry.

JEROME: She wasn't, in the end, prepared to live with a creative person. That's what it boiled down to. She wasn't prepared to fit in with the lifestyle of a creative entity. Such as myself. That's all. I'm not saying she was a selfish woman.

37

Nor am I saying she was a woman who refused to adapt or even begin to understand the pressures that – a creative person can undergo. I'm not saying that about her. After all, why should she? She's just a bloody bank manager.

ZOË: (*Sympathetically*) No. And you probably didn't understand a lot about banking, did you?

JEROME: (*Sharply*) What's that got to do with it?

ZOË: (*Quickly*) Nothing.

JEROME: Still, I'm sure she'll make some – chief clerk – a very good wife.

ZOË: (*Deciding this isn't a line worth pursuing further*) I'd love to hear some of your music. Could I, possibly?

JEROME: Yes. Perhaps. Sometime. As I say, I haven't written anything for – ages.

ZOË: Since they left?

JEROME: Nearly.

ZOË: Four years. Heavens. You really did need them, then, in some ways? Well, your muse did.

JEROME: Geain. I needed Geain. I need her back more than anything in the world.

(ZOË, *for the first time, notices the signs of his inner distress.*)

ZOË: (*Moved*) Well, I'll – do my best for you. (*Pause.*) Did she inspire your Singing Babies? I bet she did.

JEROME: *First Sounds*. Yes. (*Pause.*) I recorded her over several days . . .

ZOË: You mean it was actually her? Actually Geain you used?

JEROME: Yes. That was the first occasion I started using purely natural sounds – sampling and treating them. It took months.

ZOË: Fancy. And all that for what? Thirty seconds?

JEROME: Thirty seconds? It was a forty-five-minute piece originally.

ZOË: Oh, I see. There's more?

JEROME: Much, much, much more.

ZOË: You can't write at all, then? No ideas?

JEROME: I know what I want to write. But I don't know how to do it.

ZOË: What?

38

JEROME: (*More to himself*) I know what it's going to be. I know what I want to say. It's how to say it. I haven't got the sound. I haven't heard it. Three years and I'm still waiting to hear the sound.

ZOË: What do you want to say?

JEROME: I want to say – what I want to say is – well, I want to say – love. Really.

ZOË: (*Mystified*) Love?

JEROME: Yes.

ZOË: I see. What sort of love?

JEROME: Just – generally. Love. You know . . .

ZOË: (*Puzzled*) No, I'm not sure I –

JEROME: (*Tetchily*) Love. You've heard of love, I presume?

ZOË: Yes, yes. Sorry, only you're not putting it awfully well.

JEROME: (*Irritably*) Of course I'm not putting it awfully well. If I could put it awfully well, there wouldn't be a problem. I want to express the feeling of love in an abstract musical form. In such a way that anyone who hears it – *anyone* – no matter what language they speak – no matter what creed or colour – they will recognize it – and respond to it – and relate it to their own feelings of love that they have or they've experienced at some time – so they say – yes, my God, that's it! That's what it is! And maybe who knows, consequently, there might be a bit more of it.
(ZOË *is spellbound by this*.)

ZOË: How wonderful. (*She reflects for a second*.) It must have been a bit like this, sitting with Beethoven.

JEROME: I doubt it.

ZOË: That's how I imagine it, anyway.

JEROME: I don't think Beethoven sat down all that much. He used to stamp about the place, shouting.

ZOË: There you are, then. You're both terribly similar.
(*Pause. They have both finished their meal*.)
Oh, it must be just so awful for you. Having all those ideas and not being able to express them. Poor you.
(JEROME *looks at her*.)
I mean, I know sort of how you feel. I get that way if I'm just writing a letter. I want to say something really – I

39

don't know – heartfelt to someone. And it all comes out like the inside of some awful Christmas card. Happy tidings, boyfriend dear. At this joyous time of year. When what you mean to say is – I love you incredibly much and I'd do just about everything I could in the world to make you happy and I just want to be with you and stay close to you for ever and ever and ever – And you try and write that down so it makes sense and what do you get? Happy tidings, boyfriend dear . . . (*Aware of his gaze*) What's the matter?

JEROME: Nothing.

ZOË: Are you having second thoughts?

JEROME: No. Third thoughts.

ZOË: (*Slightly apprehensive*) Oh? What are those?

JEROME: I was just thinking – you're a very nice person, really. Only, saying it like that, I think I sound rather like one of your Christmas cards.

(*A pause.* ZOË *is a little ill at ease.*)

ZOË: I think I'll sing my song for you now, if you don't mind.

JEROME: (*Rather dismayed*) Really?

ZOË: Well, it's either that or my Shakespeare. And I don't think Queen Margaret would go down frightfully well after chicken and strawberries. (*Arranging herself*) It's all right, it's quite short . . . (*Making a false start*) You're not my – Hang on. (*She sorts out her first note.*) Right. Here we go.

    (*Sings:*) You're not my first love . . .
    It would only be a lie if I pretended –
    In the past there have been others
    Who have slept between these covers
    But I promise
    Though you're far too late in life to be my first love,
    You'll be my last love.
    I swear to you, you're gonna be my last love . . .

(*She finishes her song. Silence.*)

Well. It has this great accompaniment. Diddly-diddly diddly dom.

(*She smiles at him awkwardly.* JEROME *rises and moves to her. He stands by her, then kisses her. They break and stare at*

40

each other.)

You taste of wild strawberries.

JEROME: You taste of grouse.

(ZOË *laughs.* JEROME *smiles one of his rare smiles*.)

Do you want any more?

ZOË: More?

JEROME: Food?

ZOË: No.

JEROME: Any more anything of anything?

ZOË: (*Without hesitation*) Yes, please.

JEROME: Well, shall we . . . ? What would you prefer to do? I mean, would you like to – here? Or – ?

ZOË: I don't mind. Here's fine if – you –

JEROME: Or there's the bedroom, that might be –

ZOË: Sure. That's fine. Will she have made the bed by now, do you think?

(*She laughs*.)

JEROME: Oh, no, that's no problem. Those sheets were just for her to –

ZOË: Well, fine. Shall we go in there?

JEROME: (*Unmoving*) Yes, yes, yes.

ZOË: You want to?

JEROME: Oh, yes. You bet.

ZOË: I mean, we don't have to if you – ?

JEROME: No, no, no . . . (*Laughing*) Useful research, whatever else . . .

ZOË: (*Drawing back, concerned*) Oh, I wasn't . . . just for that.

JEROME: No, no. I was joking.

ZOË: I mean, I really want to. I don't – if I don't want to . . . I don't do that sort of thing.

JEROME: I know, I'm sure. Nor do I.

ZOË: Good. (*Pause*.) Well – shall we . . . ?

JEROME: Why not?

(*They both move towards the bedrooms. As they do,* NAN *enters clasping the section of vacuum cleaner.* ZOË *jumps.* NAN *passes them, crosses to the hall and goes out*.)

She's OK.

ZOË: I wonder. Would you think it awful of me – if I asked you

41

to switch it off?

JEROME: Switch her off?

ZOË: Just while we were – just while we were in –

JEROME: It's not very good for her, to keep switching her on and off, you see . . .

ZOË: No, no, I'm sure. It's just if it did happen to come in while we were – I think I'd probably scream or something –

JEROME: Well, I could disengage her. That would put her on standby. I'd disconnect her movement functions but leave her brain working . . .

ZOË: (*Not wanting the details*) Yes, fine. That sounds fine. I wouldn't want to damage her.

JEROME: (*Calling*) Nan, here.

NAN: (*Off*) Coming, Nan.
  (NAN *enters from the hall.*)

ZOË: Did that face come with it? I mean, is that how it came out of the factory?

JEROME: No, I – tinkered around with it. You can easily alter it, you just heat it first with a hair drier.

ZOË: Well, I think you could have chosen a better face. It looks like Mrs Danvers.

JEROME: Nan, sit.

NAN: Sitting, Nan.
  (NAN *sits.*)

JEROME: Nan, Function Command Jerome Disengage.
  (NAN *gives a slight beep.*)

NAN: Disengaged.

JEROME: Nan, walk.
  (*She gives a little beep and a twitch but stays in the chair.*)
  (*Trying again*) Nan, walk.
  (NAN *beeps and twitches again but stays still.*)
  There you are, you see. Can't move at all.

ZOË: No.
  (*She seems a little guilty at what she's requested* JEROME *to do.*)

JEROME: I'll just check – things are off.
  (*He goes to the console. He checks, unseen by* ZOË, *his*

42

recording machines. ZOË *stands in the doorway, waiting for him.* NAN's *head turns slowly and looks at her.*)

ZOË: Ah!

JEROME: What is it?

ZOË: She's just moved her head.

JEROME: Well, yes, she can still move her head. That's all right, isn't it?

ZOË: Oh yes, that's quite all right. I just wasn't expecting it. (*She starts fumbling under her dress.*)

JEROME: (*Watching her*) Are you all right?

ZOË: (*Having difficulty*) Yes, I was – I was just going to show you my – Show you my – (*She produces a string of plastic credit-type cards from her thigh wallet.*) There. Better get it over with. (*Pointing to one green card in particular among the string of others*) My Green Card. OK?

JEROME: Oh, yes . . .

ZOË: I had a full check. Last month. I'm all clear. CBH 1.

JEROME: Fine. Good. Congratulations.

ZOË: Well. You can't be too careful. Can you?

JEROME: No.
(*Slight pause.*)

ZOË: Are you – ? Have you got – ?

JEROME: Oh, yes – somewhere. It's in the – I put it in the – It's around . . .

ZOË: (*Slightly doubtful*) Good. (*Making to move*) Well . . .

JEROME: After you.

ZOË: Thank you. (*As she goes*) You still want to do this, don't you?

JEROME: (*Switching off the lights and following her*) Oh, yes . . . You bet. Rather.

ZOË: (*Off*) Because if you don't, I shan't be hurt –

JEROME: (*Off*) Oh, I do. I do. Do you?

ZOË: (*Off*) Oh, yes . . . You bet.
(*The bedroom door closes and their voices are cut off.* NAN *sits alone. She is lit, primarily from the console lights which start blinking and flashing in response to the unheard sounds in the bedroom. The light patterns become increasingly vigorous.*)

43

NAN: (*Slowly and with difficulty*) Deb–or–rah . . . Deb–or–rah . . .
(*As the lights continue to flicker on her face – blackout.*)

SCENE 2

A few hours later. It is probably morning, though it's impossible to tell. NAN *has gone.* JEROME *sits on the stool which is swivelled to one side of the console. He is working at a stretch of keyboard. He is wearing headphones, so there is no sound. He grunts occasionally to himself as he works.* NAN *swings in from the kitchen with another of her upside-down mugs of coffee. She puts it down near* JEROME.

NAN: Nice cup of cocoa. Don't let it get cold, now.
(JEROME, *even if he hears her, ignores her he is so absorbed.* NAN *returns to the kitchen. After a moment,* ZOË, *rather crumpled from sleep, comes from the bedroom wrapped in a blanket. She watches* JEROME *for a moment. She moves behind him and kisses the top of his head gently.*)

JEROME: (*Rather loudly because of his headphones*) Nan, stop! Stop that at once.
(ZOË *pulls back, hurt.* JEROME *realizes belatedly that it was unlikely to have been* NAN. *He turns and takes off the headphones.*)

ZOË: Good morning.

JEROME: Good morning.

ZOË: How long have you been up?

JEROME: (*Shrugging*) Oh . . .

ZOË: I've slept for hours.

JEROME: Yes . . .

ZOË: Well . . .

JEROME: Yes . . .

ZOË: (*Kissing him*) Good morning.

JEROME: Morning.
(ZOË *stands smiling at him. He seems rather embarrassed. There is a characteristic crash from the kitchen.*)

ZOË: (*Drily*) Mrs Danvers is up bright and early, I hear.

JEROME: Well, she's got a busy day ahead.

44

ZOË: I'm glad she didn't bring me early-morning tea.

JEROME: She's been known to. It's not an experience worth repeating. By the way, we had a visit from Rita. It's all fixed.

ZOË: Thank goodness.

JEROME: The Daughters have agreed your fine. Five hundred pounds.

ZOË: (*Aghast*) Five hundred pounds!

JEROME: It was either that or fifty lashes. I said you'd prefer the fine.

ZOË: Well, the Blaise Gillespie Agency is footing the bill for that, I can tell you. They should have warned me.

JEROME: You'll need this. (*He picks up a grubby coloured card and hands it to her.*) It's your pass card. To get you back to the railway station.

ZOË: (*Reading*) 'This is to – certify – I the undersigned have paid my debt to society.' Oh, really.

JEROME: Yes, you have to sign it, too. Don't lose it.

ZOË: I'd be a lot more impressed if they could spell 'certify'. (*She puts the card down.*)

JEROME: I'll come with you. See you off. If you'd like me to. Do you want anything? Tea or anything?

ZOË: No. I must get dressed. I need to be back by midday. I've got an audition. It's a new musical. Set in a women's prison. *Hooray for Holloway* – Well, that's what everyone's calling it, anyway. I think I'll do my song for them. What do you think?

JEROME: Sure. Why not?

(ZOË *seems reluctant to move. They stare at each other.*)

I – don't know what to say, really.

ZOË: I – was wondering. Whether I should be coming back? Whether you'd like me to come back again? I mean, sooner than – like this evening? Or tomorrow? We've still got a lot to discuss, haven't we? If we're going to get everything right for this meeting with your wife? And your daughter? What do you think? I mean, I'm not trying to push. Just as you like. What do you say?

(*A silence.*)

I don't mind. Only do say something. Please.

45

(JEROME *kisses her gently.*)
Is that a yes?

JEROME: Is that what you'd like?

ZOË: Yes.

JEROME: Then, that's what I'd like.

ZOË: Good. (*Pause.*) Just one thing.

JEROME: What?

ZOË: Who the hell is Deborah?

JEROME: (*Startled*) Who?

ZOË: Deborah. Who is she?

JEROME: No idea at all. Never heard of her.

ZOË: Well. Somebody has, that's all I can say. Mrs Danvers keeps muttering her name at me every time she passes.

JEROME: I can't think why she'd do that.

ZOË: No, right. I must just remind her of something she used to know. Her old pal, Debbie, the deep freezer perhaps. (*She watches him for a second.*) Last night, was that the first time you – you hadn't made love to anyone for some time, had you?

JEROME: Three years.

ZOË: (*Not unkindly*) Well, you'll soon get the hang of it again, I'm sure. (*Realizing she may have put this rather badly*) So. I'll get dressed. OK?

JEROME: Yes.

(*He plays with some of the knobs on the console.*)

ZOË: You all right?

JEROME: Yes.

ZOË: What were you doing? You weren't composing something, were you?

JEROME: Not really. I – er – (*He waves his hand at the console and presses a start button. From the speakers a fragment of a composition that* JEROME *has been working on. It is, recognizably,* ZOË's *laugh, recorded, sampled and re-treated in a simple, gentle, melodic line.*)

ZOË: (*Recognizing herself*) Is that me?

JEROME: Yes.

(*They listen. It is quite short. It finishes.* JEROME *stops the machine.*)

46

ZOË: That was me.

JEROME: That's right.

ZOË: When did you do that?

JEROME: While you were asleep.

ZOË: But when did you record me? Yesterday?

JEROME: That's right.

ZOË: You secretly recorded my laugh? My awful laugh?

JEROME: It's a very nice laugh.

ZOË: Watch it. I shall demand repeat fees. (*She smiles.*) It's very good.

JEROME: (*Smiling*) Thank you. It's a sketch at the moment.

ZOË: Terribly clever. It's all done with that machine?

JEROME: Yes.

ZOË: Brilliant. Brilliant machine. I'll tell you something, do you think when it goes – (*Hums a few notes*) – it wouldn't be better if it went – (*Demonstrates something different*) – don't you think?

JEROME: (*Guardedly*) How do you mean?

ZOË: Like – (*Hums her improvement again*).

JEROME: It doesn't go – (*Hums her improvement*).

ZOË: I know it doesn't. It goes – (*Hums her version of the original*).

JEROME: No, it doesn't go – (*Hums her version of the original*). It goes – (*Hums the original*).

ZOË: Well – (*Hums the original*) – then. I still think it would be better if it went – (*Hums her improvement*).

JEROME: No, it wouldn't.

ZOË: It would.

JEROME: It wouldn't.

ZOË: Why not?

JEROME: Because it doesn't go like that. That's not the way it goes.

ZOË: I know it doesn't. I'm saying, perhaps it should.

JEROME: (*Angry now*) No, it shouldn't. It goes the way it goes because it goes that way –

ZOË: Why? Why does it, necessarily?

JEROME: (*Yelling*) Because that's the way it goes, that's why. Because I wrote it that way and I'm the one that matters.

47

ZOË: (*Defensively*) All right! Yes! (*A pause.*) There's no need to shout at me. I'm not your machine, you know.

JEROME: (*Muttering*) At least she doesn't try and rewrite my music for me.

ZOË: I'm sorry. I thought you might like a suggestion. Obviously you don't. Fine. (*Pause.*) Obviously, you think that's perfect. Fine. You're the expert.

JEROME: (*Testily*) Right.

(NAN *comes from the kitchen to the hall carrying a floor-mop handle without the mop attached. She goes out busily.* ZOË *stares.*)

It's her day to mop the hall.

ZOË: Oh, good. I'm sure that floor could really do with a good scrape. Is that all you've done, then?

JEROME: What?

ZOË: Just that bit? Is that all you've written?

JEROME: No.

ZOË: Oh.

JEROME: I started a second sketch.

ZOË: Good. (*Pause.*) Well, let's hear it then. I won't say a word, I won't say a word, I promise.

JEROME: (*Reluctantly*) It's not finished.

(*He plays her the second sketch. It is, like the first, based on* ZOË *but is very different in mood – obviously this time based on a recording of* ZOË's *love sounds. She listens thunderstruck. It finishes.* JEROME *switches off the machine again.*)

ZOË: Is that what I think it is?

JEROME: Yes.

ZOË: You recorded that while we were – ?

JEROME: Yes.

ZOË: I don't believe it. You mean, while we were making love you just calmly leant out of bed and switched on a tape recorder?

JEROME: No –

ZOË: No wonder you didn't seem to have your mind on the job –

JEROME: Of course I didn't.

ZOË: Then how else did you – ?

48

JEROME: I didn't switch it on specially. They're on all the time.

ZOË: All the time?

JEROME: Yes.

ZOË: What, you mean like now?

JEROME: Yes. All the time.

ZOË: What, everywhere? In the – everywhere?

JEROME: I keep saying. Yes.

ZOË: (*Aghast*) You're sick. You're diseased. You're perverted –

JEROME: That's the way I work – That's how I work.

ZOË: Well, I'm sorry, that's not the way I work. You switch that thing off right now or I'm leaving.

JEROME: I can't switch it off. Look, it has to be on, don't you see? What's recorded here is – is what I use later. Some of it. Not all of it, obviously.

ZOË: Then you can just record parts –

JEROME: How do I know which parts to record? Jesus –

ZOË: Well, I can tell you the parts you're not going to record. You are not recording me making love, me having a bath or me in the loo – that's three for a start . . . My God, did you do this sort of thing to your wife? To your daughter?

JEROME: Yes.

ZOË: Didn't they mind? Yes, of course they minded, they walked out on you. What about Deborah, what did she have to say?

JEROME: (*Shouting*) For the tenth time, I don't know any Deborah!

(*A loud crash from the hall.*)

ZOË: Well, somebody evidently does. Why don't you ask old Mrs Danvers about her?

(*She stamps off to the bedroom.* NAN *comes from the hall, almost immediately.*)

NAN: I know what you're after, dear, and you're not going to have him. If you want Jerome, the only way you're going to get him –

JEROME: Nan, stop!

NAN: Stop, Nan.

(JEROME *stares after* ZOË. NAN *goes out to the kitchen with her mop handle.* JEROME *slides up a fader on the desk.* ZOË's

49

voice in the bedroom can be heard coming over the speakers.)

ZOË: . . . never known anything so sick in my life . . . it's disgusting . . . I mean, there is such a thing as basic privacy . . . just to record someone without even . . . I mean, recording us when we were . . . If you're recording this now, Jerome, which I presume you must be – when you play this back I want you to know that you are a sick, twisted voyeur . . . or whatever the listening equivalent is . . . an auditeur . . . a Listening Tom . . .

(*The sounds of her moving out of the bedroom.* JEROME *hastily fades down the bedroom mike.* ZOË *is heard approaching. She is finishing fastening the clothes she borrowed.*)

I was just saying, you are a Listening Tom.

JEROME: I don't know why you're suddenly behaving like this.

ZOË: If you honestly don't know, then that's probably the reason you are living on your own, Jerome.

JEROME: What are you talking about?

ZOË: I'm sorry to disappoint you but you're going to be very hard pressed, even today, to find any woman prepared to have an affair when she runs the risk of having the thing released later in stereo.

(*She makes to go.*)

JEROME: Don't forget your pass, will you?

(ZOË *returns for the card, her anger giving way to genuine hurt. As she does this,* NAN *comes from the kitchen again and stops in the doorway.*)

ZOË: God, I'm so upset, you've no idea. I really cared, you know. Did you know that? Oh, it was only supposed to be a job but I actually genuinely cared about you and your wife and your daughter and your music . . . And now, it's all been betrayed . . .

JEROME: I don't see what difference it makes.

ZOË: You can't see that there are things that people say and do with each other that they don't want other people to hear? And if they think that other people are going to be listening, then they just don't say them any more?

JEROME: But as an artist my work entirely depends on the fact that I do repeat those things –

50

ZOË: Well, then, pardon the language, but bugger your work. There are some things more important.

JEROME: Like what?

ZOË: Like me, for one. I am considerably more important than your bloody music, pardon the language. I'm sorry.

JEROME: Why? What makes you so bloody important?

ZOË: Because I'm a bloody human being, that's why. And if you can't see that, I'm sorry for you. I really am. Jerome – I know you don't like people giving you advice – but if you're still thinking of writing your piece about love, really, I should forget it.

JEROME: Thank you so much, I'll bear that in mind.

ZOË: I mean it, Jerome. Love? How could you ever possibly, ever, in a million years, conceivably describe something you can't even recognize? (*Indicating the motionless* NAN) If you don't believe me, ask her. Even she knows more about it than you do.

(ZOË *stamps out.* JEROME *stares after her. The video screen springs to life as she goes out of the front door. She glares at the camera for a second, pulls a face at it, then slams the front door. The screen blanks.*)

NAN: (*Starting to move to the hall*) I'm going to clean in here today. Don't get under my feet.

(*A thought occurs to* JEROME. *He plays with the controls on the console. Sounds of fast replay.*)

ZOË'S RECORDED VOICE: . . . for one. I am considerably more important than your bloody music, pardon the language . . .

(JEROME *spools slightly forward.*)

. . . but if you're still thinking of writing your piece about love, really, I should forget it.

JEROME'S RECORDED VOICE: Thank you so much, I'll bear that in mind.

ZOË'S RECORDED VOICE: I mean it, Jerome. Love? How could you ever poss—

(JEROME *stops the tape and spools slightly back again.*)

. . . it, Jerome. Love? How cou—

(*He plays the tape again, then winds it back by hand. Then*

51

forwards again, then back several times, playing and replaying the single word at various speeds, back and forth.)

. . . love . . . ev-ol . . . l . . o . . v . . e . . .

(JEROME *has a couple more goes, then gives up.*)

JEROME: No. Never in a million years. No truth. No sincerity. Nothing.

(*The phone rings. The screen lights up with the Department of Social Services logo.* JEROME *stares at the screen dully.*)

MERVYN'S VOICE: Mr Watkins, this is Mervyn Bickerdyke from the Department of Child Wellbeing. Calling yet again regarding a proposed meeting. This can't go on, Mr Watkins, it really can't. The time is nine o-three. Please, please, call me . . .

JEROME: Mr Bickerdyke, I would call you with pleasure, only what would be the point?

MERVYN'S VOICE: . . . my number is, as ever, on screen. Thank you.

(NAN *has entered and started to vacuum aimlessly around* JEROME's *feet, using just the disconnected telescopic tube to do so.*)

JEROME: (*Irritably*) Nan, give it a rest, please . . .

(*She stops.*)

NAN: Think I'll have a little rest.

(NAN *sits down near* JEROME. *He regards her.*)

JEROME: What do you know about love then? You pile of old junk?

(NAN *is silent.*)

(*Really for want of anything better to do*) Nan, copy.

NAN: Copying.

JEROME: Love . . .

NAN: Love . .

JEROME: (*More passionately*) Love!

NAN: Love!

JEROME: No, love!

NAN: No, love!

JEROME: (*Giving up*) . . . useless.

NAN: . . . useless.

52

(JEROME *spools the tape machine idly. He stops and plays it.*)

ZOË'S RECORDED VOICE: . . . nice name Jane. *Jane Eyre*. We did that one. I played the mad Mrs Rochester. Behind the panelling. Not much of a part. I should have played Jane, really. I'd have been really good –

(JEROME *stops the tape.*)

NAN: . . . nice name, Jane. *Jane Eyre*. We did that one. I played the mad Mrs Rochester. Behind the panelling. Not much of a part. I should have played Jane, really. I'd have been really good –

(*During this,* JEROME *looks startled for a moment. Then inspiration strikes him.*)

JEROME: Ah!

(*He goes to a cupboard under the panel. As he passes, he removes* NAN's *wig, revealing her silver skull beneath.*)

NAN: (*Echoing him*) Ah!

(*He takes from the cupboard a rolled bundle which he undoes and lays out carefully on the worktop. A neat row of electrical screwdrivers and spanners, etc., together with an open tobacco tin. Each gleaming like a surgeon's implements. He switches off a few general lights so that the illumination is concentrated around the console. He rolls up his sleeves.*)

JEROME: (*Softly, to* NAN) Well. What the hell. It's worth a try, that's what I say.

(*He selects a slender screwdriver and stands over her.*)

NAN: (*Cheerfully*) Well. What the hell. It's worth a try, that's what I say.

(JEROME *starts to remove a small grub screw from her temple. A sound as he drops the screw into the tin. The shutters clang several times as missiles strike them from outside, giving the impression of thunder.* JEROME *labours on, impervious, as – curtain.*)

53

ACT II

In the blackout, the first thing we see is LUPUS's *face on the screen.
He looks terrible. He appears to be calling from a club, judging from
the din in the background. The colour variation in the picture is also
quite extreme, veering erratically from one vivid hue to the next.*

LUPUS: (*From the screen*) Hallo, Jerry, old mate. Thought I'd
roll into view, stick my nose over your horizon there. See
how things were. I take it you're out or – busy – or
something. I'm calling from the Blue Cockatoo. Thought I
might look up one or two of the old gang, for old time's
sake. Only there doesn't seem to be anyone here, tonight.
A bit of a heavy mob round the bar – I hope this phone's
working OK, I'm not –

(*He thumps the unit in front of him, out of our vision. The
colour alters abruptly. As he continues, the lights come up on
the room. It is a week later and it is much tidier than when we
last saw it. A great effort has been made to turn the place into a
suitable home for* GEAIN. *Most of the equipment – except the
main console – has been covered up. The coffee table is partly
laid out for an informal tea party.* JEROME *comes in from the
kitchen. He, too, has made a great effort with his appearance.*)
That any better? Anyway, I'm down here at the old
Cockatoo if you feel like a jar. Since I finally lost Deborah,
I've been . . . (*Yelling to some one out of view*) Hey, keep it
down, fellows. Please?

(*He thumps the unit again. His colour changes once more.*)
Since I finally lost Deborah, I've been pretty near to – (*In
response to someone off screen*) What? What's that? And you
yours. Yes . . . (*Back in the phone*) Jesus, who are all these
guys? Anyway, as I was saying, since Deborah finally
decided to go, I've been on the verge of playing the last
waltz, I can tell you . . .

(JEROME, *as if by reflex, his mind on other things, fades*
LUPUS *down on the console.* LUPUS's *image continues to
chatter silently, changing colour once or twice more. Finally, he*

54

bangs the videophone once too often and the thing blanks out.)

JEROME: (*Calling*) Darling!

ZOË'S VOICE: (*From the kitchen*) Hallo, darling?

JEROME: Darling, what are you doing?

ZOË'S VOICE: (*Off*) I'm just finishing off in here, darling.

JEROME: Darling, come on in, they've arrived.

ZOË'S VOICE: (*Off*) Right you are, darling. Just a tick.

(*A moment later and* ZOË *comes on. Or rather it is* NAN *made over into a version of* ZOË. *She looks a good deal like* ZOË *but still has* NAN's *distinctive walk – and several of* NAN's *old mannerisms which emerge from time to time. One improvement* JEROME *seems to have wrought is that she is carrying a plate of sandwiches the right way up. She, too, is very smartly dressed in the usual long frock and with a great deal of ribbons and bows in her new wig.* JEROME *has also rather emphasized her figure. She's a degree more voluptuous than* ZOË *and more shapely than* NAN. *She looks rather like a parody of an old-style Southern belle.*)

NAN: (*Brightly, as she enters*) Hallo! Hallo! Hallo! Welcome! Welcome! Welcome! Sorry. I completely lost track of the time. Typical.

(*She puts the sandwiches down on the coffee table.* JEROME *watches anxiously.*)

JEROME: Good. Good girl. That's it. Darling, will you fetch the tea, or shall I?

NAN: I'll fetch the tea, darling. Excuse me.

(*She goes off.* JEROME *watches her critically.*)

JEROME: (*Muttering*) There's nothing I can do with that leg.

NAN: (*From the kitchen*) Just coming, everyone.

(*A crash from the kitchen.*)

(*Off*) Oh, for goodness' sake, you extremely stupid old bat. Who put that there, then?

JEROME: Oh, for God's sake – (*Calling angrily*) Darling!

NAN: (*Off, sweetly*) Yes, darling.

JEROME: Darling, come here, you scrapheap.

NAN: (*Off*) Coming, darling.

(NAN *returns, empty-handed.* JEROME *gets out a small screwdriver from his tool kit.*)

55

JEROME: (*Brusquely*) Darling, sit down.

NAN: (*Sitting*) Sitting down, darling.

(JEROME *selects a screwdriver and approaches* NAN.)

JEROME: (*Muttering*) They're going to be here in a minute, you useless heap. Darling, disengage.

(NAN *beeps and sits immobile in the chair as* JEROME *lies on his back on the floor and disappears under her skirt.*)

(*Slightly muffled, to himself really*) Sorry to switch you off but I'm not getting a hundred volts through me again. Yes . . . I keep adjusting this balance control but – it's such – fine . . . tuning . . . I think it's this leg of yours – you keep shaking your works about . . . Darling, engage.

(NAN *beeps again.*)

NAN: Reconnected. Operational seventy-eight point seven four. We are twenty-one point two six per cent unstable and are within three point seven four per cent of permanent shutdown.

(*She beeps.* JEROME *emerges again.*)

JEROME: Don't you dare shut down on me. Not now. Darling, walk about.

NAN: Yes, darling.

(*She does so.*)

JEROME: That's better, that's better. Precious!

(NAN *comes immediately and kisses his cheek. She waltzes away again.*)

(*An experimental laugh*) Ha! Ha!

(NAN *responds with one of* ZOË's *laughs.*)

Good. (*Calling again*) Precious!

(NAN *comes and kisses him on the cheek again, then moves away.*)

Good! Ha! Ha!

(NAN *laughs again.* JEROME *moves away to one side of her.*)

(*In a normal tone*) Zoë . . .

(NAN's *head turns to look at him, as if listening. She is programmed to do this whenever her name is mentioned.* JEROME *moves to the other side of her.*)

(*As before*) Zoë . . .

(NAN *looks at him again.*)

56

(*Rather amazed*) It works. Darling, it works!

NAN: It works, darling!

JEROME: Nan, still –

(NAN *ignores him*.)

I mean, darling, still.

(NAN *stops still*.)

NAN: Still, darling.

JEROME: Let me straighten your wig. Here . . . (*Studying her*) I don't think I've got your mouth right even now.

(*He adjusts her appearance, trying to remould her face with his thumbs. The doorbell rings. JEROME jumps. The screen lights up to show CORINNA and MERVYN waiting at the front door.*) Here we go, then. Darling, kitchen.

NAN: Yes, darling.

(*She starts to go*.)

JEROME: No, no. Wait. (*He moves to the console*.) Darling, here.

NAN: Coming, darling.

JEROME: (*Standing her in front of the screen where she can study CORINNA and MERVYN*) Darling, register.

NAN: Register, darling.

JEROME: Not child. Not child.

NAN: Not child. Registered, Nan.

JEROME: Good. Darling, kitchen.

NAN: Kitchen, darling.

JEROME: Darling, take the plate.

NAN: I'll take the plate, darling.

(NAN *takes up the plate and goes off to the kitchen*. JEROME *straightens his appearance. The doorbell rings again*.)

CORINNA'S VOICE: (*Impatiently, through the speakers*) Jerome, come on, open the door. Please.

JEROME: Here we go. Those warm vibrant tones . . .

(JEROME *presses the door button. They remain out there*.)

CORINNA'S VOICE: Jerome! For heaven's sake!

JEROME: Push the door! Push it!

(*The doorbell rings again*.)

MERVYN'S VOICE: (*From the speakers*) Mr Watkins!

CORINNA'S VOICE: Jerome!

JEROME: Push the bloody thing – ! Oh, for goodness' sake . . .

57

(*He runs out down the hall. We see, on the video screen, him opening the door to them.*)

CORINNA'S VOICE: (*From the speakers, sarcastically*) Well, thank you so much.

JEROME'S VOICE: (*From the speakers*) Come in, then, come in.

MERVYN'S VOICE: (*From the speakers*) How do you do, Mr Watkins. Mervyn Bickerdyke of Child Wellbeing.

CORINNA'S VOICE: (*From the speakers*) Yes, come on, let's get out of this hideous hall first . . .

(*The screen blanks as they all come inside and the door closes. The sound of them approaching down the hall.* CORINNA *enters first, followed closely by* JEROME. MERVYN *follows behind them.* CORINNA *is, of course, very similar in looks to the original* NAN *but with little of* NAN's *submissive nature and a good deal more personal aura, not to mention neuroses. In her mid-thirties, she is formally dressed as though for a business meeting rather than a social event.* MERVYN *is about the same age. One of those big, gentle, good-natured, pleasant men, he obviously gets by in his job through kindness and tact and by offending no one – rather than through dynamic personality. At present, he is filled with a nervousness which he can't altogether conceal.*)

JEROME: (*As they enter*) . . . I can't help it, there's a fault with the door . . .

CORINNA: There was a fault with the door when I left . . .

JEROME: Probably because you slammed it so hard when you went, dear.

MERVYN: Hallo, Mr Watkins, my name is –

CORINNA: If I slammed it, I had very just cause.

JEROME: (*Aware someone is missing*) Where's Geain?

CORINNA: If anyone had reason to slam a door . . .

MERVYN: Mr Watkins, I think I ought to introduce myself – I'm . . .

JEROME: Where the hell's Geain? What have you done with Geain?

CORINNA: Geain is coming.

JEROME: What have you done with her?

CORINNA: She is coming. Geain is coming.

58

JEROME: When? Because I'm not meeting without her. There's to be no meeting without Geain.

MERVYN: Mr Watkins, if I could just nudge my way in a moment to introduce myself –

CORINNA: Geain went on in the car to buy something. She'll be here in a minute. Anyway, we need to talk without her first –

JEROME: You left that child out there in a car on her own – ?

CORINNA: Jerome, don't be ridiculous. She is not on her own. It is an armour-plated limousine which cost a fortune to hire – but since that's the only way we could guarantee to get to this place these days . . . She has the driver with her and a man riding – whatever it's called – riding sidegun –

MERVYN: Shotgun.

CORINNA: Shotgun. Thank you, Mr Bickerdyke. Besides which, she is thirteen years old and quite capable of looking after herself.

MERVYN: I would endorse that, Mr Watkins.

JEROME: (*Slightly pacified*) I'm not agreeing anything without Geain having the chance to say what she feels.

CORINNA: I've no doubt she will. Don't worry.

(*A slight pause as* CORINNA *inspects the place.* MERVYN *seizes his chance.*)

MERVYN: Look, I'm going to nip right in there for a second, just to say hallo, my name is Merv –

CORINNA: I must say this place is looking remarkably tidy. You must have been scrubbing at it for weeks.

JEROME: Well, we wouldn't want you picking up any nasty germs whilst you were visiting us, would we?

CORINNA: Us?

JEROME: What? (*A great show of having forgotten.*) Oh, dear. Oh, heavens. Ah. How could I have forgotten? You haven't met Zoë, have you?

CORINNA: Zoë?

JEROME: Zoë.

CORINNA: Who or what is Zoë?

JEROME: Zoë is my – fiancée.

CORINNA: Fiancée?

59

JEROME: Yes.

MERVYN: Oh. Many congratulations.

JEROME: (*To* MERVYN) Thank you very much.

CORINNA: Did you say fiancée?

JEROME: Yes.

CORINNA: I don't believe it. This is a joke – This is an obscene, grotesque joke. A fiancée . . . ?

JEROME: Before you meet her, dearest, could I ask you, please – she is very sweet, rather shy – and a little unused to strangers . . . So, please, don't try and be clever with her or embarrass her with awkward questions . . . because she couldn't cope with that. All right? Would that be remotely possible, do you think?

CORINNA: I don't believe any of this. Not one word.

JEROME: (*Calling*) Darling!

NAN'S VOICE: (*From the kitchen*) Hallo, darling?

CORINNA: My God!

JEROME: Darling, what are you doing?

NAN: (*Off*) I'm just finishing off in here, darling.

JEROME: Darling, come on in, they've arrived.

NAN: (*Off*) Right you are, darling. Just a tick.

CORINNA: (*Rather shaken*) Well, this – certainly does alter things. Doesn't it?

JEROME: (*Smiling*) Doesn't it?

(NAN *comes in as before.*)

NAN: (*Brightly, as she enters*) Hallo! Hallo! Hallo! Welcome! Welcome! Welcome! Sorry. I completely lost track of the time. Typical.

(CORINNA *and* MERVYN *gape.*)

JEROME: Darling, this is Corinna.

NAN: Hallo. Corinna. I've heard so much about you.

CORINNA: (*Faintly*) Have you?

(MERVYN *has never seen anyone quite like her.* JEROME *is a little easier, now that he is past the first hurdle.*)

JEROME: Well, now. I'm sure we'd all like some tea, wouldn't we? Darling, will you fetch the tea, or shall I?

NAN: I'll fetch the tea, darling. Excuse me.

MERVYN: (*Stepping forward to* NAN, *hand extended*) Hallo, may

60

I just say hallo. My name is . . .
(NAN *sweeps past him, unaware. He jumps back*.)
CORINNA: Are you telling me that she's living here voluntarily?
JEROME: Of course she is. We're engaged.
CORINNA: Living with *you*?
JEROME: Why not?
CORINNA: But she's – she's –
MERVYN: Very much so. Congratulations again.
CORINNA: Where did you meet her?
JEROME: She's an actress.
MERVYN: (*Impressed*) Really?
JEROME: A classical actress.
CORINNA: Classical?
(NAN *comes back in unexpectedly. She is empty-handed*.)
NAN: (*Brightly, as she enters*) Hallo! Hallo! Hallo! Welcome!
Welcome! Welcome! Sorry. I –
JEROME: (*Interrupting swiftly*) Darling, the tea!
NAN: (*Unflustered*) I'll fetch the tea, darling. Excuse me.
(*She goes out. A pause*.)
JEROME: Excuse me.
(*He hurries out after* NAN *to the kitchen*.)
CORINNA: I think she's wearing one of my old dresses.
MERVYN: Oh, yes?
CORINNA: She's certainly made herself at home here.
JEROME: (*From the kitchen, shouting fiercely*) Darling, tea!
Darling, tea!
NAN: (*From the kitchen, equally fiercely*) Darling, tea! Darling,
tea!
(*Several loud clangs. The others stare.* JEROME *hurries back*.)
JEROME: Sorry. Just – lending her a hand. Please, sit down.
(*They sit. Silence.* JEROME *listens anxiously. He rises. Then
sits again*.)
CORINNA: Does she need any help?
JEROME: No, no.
(NAN *returns. She carries the tea pot and a plate of small
cakes*.)
NAN: (*To the seated assembly*) Do sit down, everyone.
MERVYN: (*Rising apologetically*) Sorry, I . . .

61

NAN: Nice pot of tea.

JEROME: Oh, super. Clever little cuddles.

NAN: And some home-made cakes.

JEROME: (*Rather over-enthusiastically*) Home-made cakes! Wonderful! Wonderful! Yummy, yummy, yum-yum.

MERVYN: You made these yourself?

JEROME: Yes, she did. Didn't you, darling, you made these yourself?

NAN: I made them myself, darling. (*She grabs the tea pot rather jerkily.*) Tea, everyone?

JEROME: (*Hastily taking the tea pot from her*) I'll pour the tea. (*As he pours*) You relax. You've been at it all day. Precious. (NAN *rises at once and kisses him on the cheek.*) (*Rather coyly*) Oh, come on. Not in front of everyone . . . (*He laughs.* NAN *laughs in response.* CORINNA *stares in disbelief.*)

CORINNA: I think I'm going to be sick.

JEROME: (*To the others*) She's been at it all day. Slaving away in that kitchen. Then she was up at dawn, scouring the place from top to bottom. She never stops. All day. Now, do we want milk or lemon? (*To* NAN) Darling, you won't have anything, I take it.

NAN: I won't have anything, I take it, darling.

JEROME: (*To the others*) Eats nothing at all. Fierce diet.

CORINNA: (*Rather sourly*) Doesn't look as if she needs to bother.

JEROME: She doesn't. Wonderful metabolism. Milk?

CORINNA: Lemon.

MERVYN: I'll have milk, thank you.
(JEROME *finishes serving the tea, helping himself as he does so.*)
Could I stick a foot in the door here just to take this opportunity to say hallo, formally? I'm Mervyn Bickerdyke, Child Wellbeing, of course. I spoke to you on the phone, Mr Watkins. Eventually.

JEROME: Yes, so you did. Sandwich?

MERVYN: Thank you. (*Smiling at* NAN) Seeing as they were made with your own fair hands.
(NAN *ignores him.* CORINNA *grabs a sandwich, irritably.*)

62

I'm sorry. After you, after you.

(*All, except* NAN, *help themselves to sandwiches.*)

We were just hearing, Zoë, that you were an actress.

CORINNA: Classical, is that right?

JEROME: That's right, isn't it, darling? You're a classical actress, aren't you, little blossom?

NAN: Oh yes. Arkadina in Chekhov and Queen Margaret in *See How They Run.*

CORINNA: (*Puzzled*) Really?

JEROME: That was the – Royal Shakespeare production, of course –

MERVYN: Of course. Now, to the reason we've all met – (*Something starts to bleep somewhere about his person.* JEROME *checks* NAN *nervously.*) – we've . . . Oh. Would you excuse me. My bleeper. (*He rises.*)

JEROME: (*Waving towards the console*) Do you want to make a – ?

MERVYN: No, no. I have my portable here. Thank you very much.

(MERVYN *moves away from them to a far corner of the room. He produces a wafer-thin pocket phone from his jacket and answers his call. He stops bleeping. He murmurs indistinctly while the others continue their tea.*)

CORINNA: Well, I have to confess, Jerome, that I am simply amazed. I didn't think anyone could do it, Zoë. Make a civilized animal out of this man.

(*She laughs.* NAN *laughs in response.*)

JEROME: I'm putty in her hands, darling, aren't I, precious?

NAN: Aren't you, precious?

(*She gets up and kisses him on the cheek and sits again.* CORINNA *glares at them, disgusted by this blissful scene.*)

CORINNA: Don't think I don't know why you're doing this, both of you. Trying to impress that – (*Indicating* MERVYN) – limp lettuce over there . . . God, he's wet. Three hours we were in that car with him bleating away. That's when his bleeper wasn't going. He was either bleeping or bleating, like a radio-controlled sheep. God, I despair of

63

men these days, I despair. They're all so lank. And dank.

JEROME: (*To* NAN) My ex-wife airing her views in general.

CORINNA: Well, ask Zoë. I bet you she feels the same. Zoë, outside this very special little love-nest, this haven of domestic fervour, don't you find most men these days utterly spineless and flaccid? I mean, that's just talking to them – I'm not even talking about bed. Don't you agree, Zoë?

(NAN *looks blank.*)

Yes, she does. She's just being loyal, poor thing.

JEROME: She knows when to keep quiet, don't you, Zoë?

CORINNA: She'd need to. Living with you.

(*She laughs.* NAN, *responding to this laughs too.* CORINNA *looks at her rather sharply, sizing up her rival afresh.*)

Yes, you're a deep one, aren't you, Zoë? Quite a lot going on in there, I imagine.

JEROME: You bet.

(MERVYN *finishes the call and rejoins them.*)

MERVYN: Sorry. Never far away from the office when you've got one of those.

(*He waves his phone.*)

CORINNA: I thought you said you had two of them?

MERVYN: Ah, yes. I have my private home phone as well. In case my wife wants to get hold of me.

CORINNA: (*Sweetly*) But that one doesn't ring very often, I imagine?

MERVYN: (*Missing that*) Right. Where were we? Yes. Young Geain –

JEROME: Look, if we're going to start talking, I think Zoë would rather – get on with other things.

CORINNA: Oh, surely not?

JEROME: Well, she was saying earlier she felt she'd feel a bit in the way. And she does have some work to get on with. Darling, if you want to go and study now . . .

NAN: (*Rising at once*) I want to go and study now, darling.

(*She goes out to the bedrooms.*)

CORINNA: No, no, this is ridiculous, she must stay. Zoë! (*To* JEROME) Jerome, tell her to come back at once, for

64

heaven's sake, she needs to hear all this.

JEROME: No, she really does need to do some work. She has a big audition tomorrow.

MERVYN: Really? What's that for?

JEROME: For a musical.

MERVYN: (*More impressed still*) Does she sing as well?

JEROME: Like an angel.

CORINNA: How else? None the less, if she really is intending to live here with you, possibly even marry you – God help her – she ought to be in on the discussions –

MERVYN: It would be advisable.

JEROME: (*Reluctantly*) Well. For a few minutes. (*Calling*) Darling!

NAN: (*Off*) Hallo, darling!

JEROME: (*Calling*) Darling, come back.

NAN: (*Off*) Right you are, darling, just a tick.

JEROME: She's coming.

MERVYN: (*Indicating the sandwiches*) May I – ?
     (JEROME *waves for him to go ahead.* MERVYN *evidently enjoys his food.*)

CORINNA: Has she hurt her leg?

JEROME: What?

CORINNA: She appears to be limping.

JEROME: Oh, she damaged it – while she was rushing around dancing.

MERVYN: She dances as well?

JEROME: No one to touch her . . .

CORINNA: I'm longing to see her fly.
     (NAN *re-enters.*)

NAN: (*Brightly, as she enters*) Hallo! Hallo! Hallo! Welc–

JEROME: (*Cutting her off*) Darling, we want you to sit here with us.

NAN: (*Sitting*) Yes, darling.

MERVYN: Maybe we can persuade you to sing for us before we leave, Zoë.

JEROME: I'm afraid not.

MERVYN: No?

JEROME: No. She's saving the voice.

65

MERVYN: Oh, I see.

JEROME: Professionals. They have to be very careful how often they sing.

CORINNA: Or even speak, apparently.

(*She smiles at* NAN.)

MERVYN: Well. I think we ought to – make a start, then. The question we have to decide first, regarding Geain, is whether – (*He starts to beep again.*) I'm sorry. Please excuse me –

CORINNA: (*Exasperated*) Oh, dear God.

MERVYN: Don't worry, I'll put them on to answer. It's the office again, I'll put them on to answer.

(*He fumbles in another pocket as he continues to beep.*)

JEROME: (*Intrigued*) You have an answering machine on you as well?

CORINNA: If you turn him upside down, he also makes ice-cream.

MERVYN: (*Rather proudly*) I've got a few wires about my person, yes, I have to admit it. (*He finds his answering machine and switches it on. The beeping stops. Producing items from various pockets and holding them up to show them*) Answering machine. Neat, eh? Home phone. Office phone. Oh, this is an interesting one. Location finder. If you're ever hopelessly lost. Switch it on and it can pinpoint your on-ground position to within twelve square metres. French. Of course. Then you've got this – excuse me. (*He takes off his jacket to reveal that the whole of his neck and arms are encased in a criss-cross of wires.*) This is a personal alarm system. Latest type. West German. Naturally. Made by Heisser-Hausen Zeiplussen. They're a subsidiary of Glotz.

JEROME: (*Vaguely*) Oh, yes.

MERVYN: Any physical attack on my person and this thing screams the place down.

CORINNA: Do you need a machine to do it for you?

MERVYN: (*Putting on his jacket again*) Ah, but what if I was rendered unconscious? I couldn't scream at all, could I? Whereas this thing. Two kilometre radius – up to an hour, guaranteed. And it automatically phones the police.

66

CORINNA: And you certainly couldn't do that if you were unconscious, could you? Must take you ages getting dressed in the morning.

MERVYN: Maybe. But I can get undressed quick enough, if called upon to do so, don't you worry about that.

(*He laughs at his own roguish wit.* CORINNA *looks at him coldly.* NAN *responds, laughing.*)

(*Winking at* NAN *as he sits again*) Sorry. Mustn't get me on to these things. Fatal. My hobby, rather.

JEROME: Have some more to eat.

MERVYN: Thank you.

(*He helps himself.*)

CORINNA: Lovely home-made cakes, Zoë. Clever you. Very, very like those new deep-frozen ones you bake in the packet. But yours are twice as good.

(*She smiles at* NAN *again.*)

MERVYN: Getting back to Geain, then. We mustn't get sidetracked, must we? We –

(*The phone rings in the room.*)

Ignore it. Ignore that. I'm on answer, ignore it.

JEROME: That's my phone.

MERVYN: Oh, is it? Yes, of course, that's your phone . . .

(*He laughs.* NAN *laughs as well.*)

CORINNA: That woman laughs at anything.

JEROME: She's got a sense of humour. That's why I love her. Don't I, precious?

(NAN *kisses him.*)

CORINNA: Oh, do stop it, both of you.

(*The answering machine picks up the incoming call. On screen,* LUPUS *appears. He is still in the club phone box but there seems to be some sort of riot going on round him. There also appears to be something on fire, judging from the smoke and the flames reflected on his face. He looks somewhat the worse for wear.*)

My God, it's not him . . .

LUPUS: Hi, Jerry, mate. I'll have to make this a quick one. Lupus, still at the old Cockatoo. I hope the answering machine doesn't mean you're on your way here. Anyway, this is to say, if you do get this message, don't bother coming down. It's got a bit rough here . . .

(JEROME *gets up and crosses to the console.*)

JEROME: Excuse me.

LUPUS: Apparently, this afternoon the club was booked by two hundred members of the Motorhead Nostalgic Appreciation Society. I ask you, Jerry – Motorhead! Where have they been? I said to one of them, listen, if it's nostalgia you're into then do yourself a favour, treat yourself to the Moody Blues and listen to real music. I mean, really –

(*His voice is cut off as* JEROME *fades him down.*)

CORINNA: Good old Lupus.

MERVYN: Do you need to make any calls on his behalf? His lawyer or something? It looked quite serious . . .

JEROME: No, no. He's all right. That's always happening to Lupus. Nothing out of the ordinary.

(*On screen, the phone booth topples on to its side.* LUPUS *goes with it, still gesticulating and talking. None of them notices this. The screen goes blank.*)

There you are, you see, he's hung up.

CORINNA: The man is a walking state of emergency. Is he still with that woman? With Deborah?

(NAN *makes a little strangled sound.*)

Or is she off with somebody else's husband again?

JEROME: I really wouldn't know. Look, let's –

CORINNA: Dear little Deborah, I wonder how she is these days?

(NAN *reacts again and does so every time Deborah's name is mentioned.*)

Heard anything from Deborah lately, have you, Zoë?

JEROME: I don't think Zoë wants to talk about Deborah and nor do I.

CORINNA: I'm sure you don't. But how do you know Zoë doesn't?

JEROME: Because she doesn't.

CORINNA: Have you asked her? Ask her.

MERVYN: (*Jocularly*) I think I'd quite like to hear about Deborah from the sound of things . . .

68

(*He laughs.* NAN *laughs.* JEROME *glares at him.*)

CORINNA: Go on. Ask her.

JEROME: There isn't the faintest chance is there, darling, you want to hear about Deborah?

NAN: I want to hear about Deborah, darling.

CORINNA: (*Scenting blood*) There you are. I told you she did. Of course she does. Everyone should know about Deborah, shouldn't they? The Deborahs of this world need discussing. They need a constant airing – in her case, literally. Zoë needs to know. Forewarned is forearmed. And I'm sure Mr Bickerdyke here, who can get undressed very, very quickly if called upon to do so, might like to be warned about Deborah, too.

JEROME: Look, come on, Corinna, why drag that up again . . .

MERVYN: I think we might be in essence be straying away from the basic issues here . . . (*He beeps again.*) Ignore that. Ignore that! That is me, this time, that is definitely me.

CORINNA: (*Confidentially, to* NAN) Never mind, Zoë. Later, when we're alone, darling, I'll tell you all about Deborah. (*She laughs.*)

NAN: (*Laughing*) You'll tell me all about Deborah, darling.

CORINNA: I think Zoë and I have a lot more in common than I thought.

JEROME: I don't think Zoë has anything to say to you at all.

CORINNA: What's the matter? Frightened she might hear the truth?

JEROME: Not at all.

CORINNA: That's a man's greatest nightmare, isn't it? All the women in his life getting together and talking about him. What's he like at breakfast, darling? What's he like in bed?

NAN: He'll soon get the hang of it again, I'm sure.

(CORINNA *blinks.*)

CORINNA: What did she say?

(JEROME *laughs loudly.* NAN *follows suit.*)

JEROME: God, this girl's sense of humour is wicked sometimes. Wicked. Isn't it, precious?

(NAN *kisses him.* CORINNA *is very puzzled.*)

CORINNA: (*Staring at them both*) Yes . . .

69

MERVYN: I think if I could hop, step and jump in again at this point. Just – looking at the time . . .

CORINNA: Listen, we can keep this very simple. The situation is this. Geain has reached an age now when I am more than happy for us both to share responsibility, Jerome. I am happy that she sees you. I am happy that she spends time with you.

JEROME: You what?

CORINNA: My only –

JEROME: You are saying this now, after – ?

CORINNA: My only –

JEROME: After four years of – ?

CORINNA: May I please finish? My only misgiving has been the thought of Geain coming to see you here. The combination of you, the flat and the general state of this neighbourhood always seemed to me strong enough reason to prevent her coming. Well, the neighbourhood certainly hasn't improved but – thanks I suspect to Zoë, quite a lot else has. So I withdraw my objections. Geain may come and see you if she likes, whenever she likes.

JEROME: Do you hear that, Mr Bickerdyke?

MERVYN: Yes, indeed.

JEROME: You are bearing witness to this?

MERVYN: I am.

JEROME: Well. That's that, isn't it?

CORINNA: Presumably. It's up to Geain. That's if Mr Bickerdyke has no objections?

JEROME: You don't have objections?

MERVYN: No, no . . .

JEROME: There's no problem, is there?

MERVYN: Well . . .

JEROME: What?

MERVYN: There is one aspect with which I'm not entirely happy, I have to confess. I mean, although the youngster has to come first, indeed her interests are of paramount importance – everyone, in a sense, needs to be considered. And I'm not altogether convinced that there aren't certain individuals – certain aspects of the existing – (*He beeps. In*

70

time, he goes on to 'answer'.) – ignore that – please – ignore that – aspects of the existing status quo that could suffer – as the result of any subsequent modified arrangements – regarding the possible – alteration of the present – custodianship of the youngster. As of this present time. (CORINNA *makes a loud snoring noise.*)
If you follow me.

JEROME: Do I take it you are not happy for Geain to come here?

MERVYN: Well . . .

JEROME: You don't consider us suitable?

MERVYN: It's difficult to put into words . . .

JEROME: I'm her father.

MERVYN: Oh, quite.

JEROME: And Zoë loves children. She adores them. She was saying so only the other day. Tell them your feelings towards children.
(*A slight pause.* NAN *does not react.*)
(*Remembering the key word*) Sweetheart.

NAN: (*Promptly*) I'd love to have children of my own. Wouldn't it be lovely to hear them rushing about the flat, laughing and yelling? With the right man – someone who'd share them – they'd be everything I ever wanted. I suppose you're either maternal or you aren't. I know which I am.
(*A silence.*)

JEROME: (*Moved*) Darling, thank you.

NAN: Thank you, darling.

MERVYN: (*Rather moved*) Well, what can one say . . . ?

CORINNA: What indeed?

MERVYN: I'll be honest with you, Mr Watkins. What I've experienced here this afternoon has been for me – as a married man myself – heart-warming. You and your – fiancée – Zoë – well – you can feel it when you walk in the door. You can almost sense the happiness.

JEROME: There you are, then.

MERVYN: It's just that I'm a little afraid of what might happen if we introduced Geain into this house. There is, on the one hand, the real hope that your own happiness could have a

71

beneficial effect on the youngster –

JEROME: It's bound to.

MERVYN: Ah, but it has been known to happen, that because the couple were so contented, the introduction of the youngster actually upset the happy status quo. And the couple became unhappy as a result of having the youngster with them. Consequently, the youngster was no longer in a happy home but an unhappy one. Which naturally in turn made it, the youngster, feel guilty because it felt responsible for causing that unhappiness. Which had the knock-on effect, of course, of making the youngster unhappy, which won't do at all. Because, after all, the bottom line is the happiness of the youngster, is it or is it not, correct me if I'm wrong?

(*A pause. They stare at him, trying to work out what he's said.*)

CORINNA: Your job's a good deal more complicated than most people imagine, isn't it, Mr Bickerdyke?

JEROME: You feel that Geain might upset me and Zoë?

MERVYN: I'm saying she could. At her present stage of adolescence. Which is – complex.

JEROME: And that, in turn, would upset Geain?

MERVYN: It's possible.

JEROME: Well, that's simple enough. If that happens I'll get rid of her.

MERVYN: I beg your pardon?

JEROME: I'll get rid of her.

MERVYN: Get rid of Geain?

JEROME: No, of course not. Not Geain. I'll get rid of Zoë. That's easy enough.

MERVYN: (*Stunned*) You'd get rid of her?

JEROME: Yes. We'd – you know – split up. For the sake of the child.

MERVYN: Just like that?

CORINNA: What does Zoë have to say about that?

JEROME: Darling, you wouldn't mind us splitting up for the sake of the child?

NAN: I wouldn't mind us splitting up for the sake of the child, darling.

72

JEROME: There you are, you see, she doesn't mind at all.

MERVYN: But that's what you did before.

JEROME: What?

MERVYN: You and your wife. That's what you did before. That's the root of the problem now. You can't do that again. Think of the youngster. We must think of the youngster, Mr Watkins.

JEROME: Yes, that was with her mother. That was different. I mean, this is only with – only – with –

(*A pause.*)

CORINNA: Only some woman or other, he was going to say.

JEROME: No.

CORINNA: Well, Zoë. You're taking this all very calmly, dear. I hope you know what you're doing. Personally, I'd have punched your precious fiancé on the nose.

(NAN *kisses* JEROME *on the cheek.*)

Oh well, save your breath. Never mind, Zoë, if you're very good in this life, you might just come back in the next as a shoe-cleaning kit. You'll enjoy that.

JEROME: There is no need to be offensive, Corinna. Just because the sight of two people completely and hopelessly in love distresses you, there's –

CORINNA: In love? Jerome, you are treating this woman like a doormat. How dare you? And Zoë, for heaven's sake, darling, stand up for yourself.

(NAN *stands up.*)

NAN: (*Swiftly*) Standing up, darling.

JEROME: (*Swiftly*) Darling, sit down.

NAN: (*Sitting*) Sitting down, darling.

MERVYN: Listen, I must just be allowed to finish the point I started making . . . Which is, that this is all a big hypothetical if. Much more likely is that Geain will respond to the peaceful friendly ambience and the reverse will happen. The relationship between the three of you will take root and blossom . . .

NAN: Oh, yes. Arkadina in Chekhov and Queen Margaret in *See How They Run*.

MERVYN: I beg your pardon?

73

CORINNA: What?

JEROME: She wants to go and study. Darling, you need to go and study.

NAN: (*Rising immediately*) I need to go and study, darling.
(NAN *goes off to the bedrooms.*)

MERVYN: Do you think you may have offended her?

CORINNA: Impossible.

MERVYN: I don't know, some people may not care to be referred to as shoe-cleaning equipment.

CORINNA: Oh, surely not in Zoë's case? Living with Jerome, that comes under the heading of a compliment.
(MERVYN *looks at his watch.*)

MERVYN: They're rather late, aren't they? I think I might phone the car. Do you think that would be an idea? Make sure they're all right?

CORINNA: If you like.

JEROME: Do you want to use the – (*Indicating his phone*)?

MERVYN: No, no. I'll use my other line. It's quite all right.
(*He moves off to the hall to speak in private.*)

CORINNA: Well. Congratulations, Jerome. I'm very, very, very pleased for you. I'm delighted. (*Pause.*) I'm so thrilled, you've no idea. (*Pause.*) No, really, I am. I'm being perfectly sincere. (*Pause.*) At least one of us has managed to . . . (*Pause.*) I'm really pleased. Honestly. You must be – so happy. (*Pause.*) You're very lucky, both of you. (*Pause.*) She's lovely and obviously wonderful for you and you're both very much in love. (*Pause.*) Who could ask for anything more?

JEROME: I couldn't.
(*He smiles.*)

CORINNA: No.
(*A pause.*)
(*With sudden suppressed fury.*) You smug bastard.
(MERVYN *returns from the hall.*)

MERVYN: Sorry to interrupt . . . They're here. The car's just arrived. Apparently, they were –
(*He is cut short by the doorbell ringing. The face of a short-haired, dark-chinned hermaphrodite appears on the screen.*)

74

MERVYN: Ah, I'll get it. I'll get it.
  (*He goes out to the hall again.*)
JEROME: No, don't open the door without . . . (*Seeing what is on the screen*) No, don't open it. Don't let that thing in here.
  (*On screen,* MERVYN *opens the door.*)
  What's he doing? (*Diving for his swordstick*) What's that idiot think he's doing? He's letting in every monster in the neighbourhood.
CORINNA: Jerome, dear. That is Geain.
JEROME: What?
  (GEAIN *enters the flat and closes the door. The screen blanks.*)
CORINNA: That's your daughter. That's Geain. Remember?
JEROME: (*Stunned*) Geain? That is Geain?
  (GEAIN *enters. In the flesh, she looks if anything slightly more grotesque. She wears a not unfamiliar parody of male work clothes circa 1955. But hers are carried to some extreme. Heavy boots, cord trousers with a wide leather belt, padded rather incongruously at the crotch, old, faded shirt open at the neck to reveal the currently fashionable 'hairy vest' i.e. an undershirt knotted with a mass of supposed chest hair. The back of her jacket is studded with the words:* SONS OF BITCHES. *Her hair is short, brushed straight back and oiled; her only make-up the blue-chinned, unshaven look.*)
GEAIN: (*Cursorily*) 'llo.
  (*She strides into the room, picks up a sandwich and sits, without ceremony or introduction.* JEROME *stares, thunderstruck. Her brusqueness, one suspects, also hides a shyness.*)
CORINNA: Here she is.
GEAIN: (*Scowling*) He.
CORINNA: Sorry, my mistake. He. You remember your – son Geain, don't you? This is your father, dear.
GEAIN: (*Nodding to* JEROME) 'llo.
  (JEROME *manages to open and shut his mouth.* GEAIN *crams another sandwich into her mouth.*)
MERVYN: (*With inappropriate avuncularity*) Did you manage to buy that game you were looking for, Geain?
GEAIN: (*Scowling*) No.

75

MERVYN: Oh, why was that?

GEAIN: (*Muttering*) Daughters.

MERVYN: What's that?

GEAIN: Daughters.

MERVYN: Tortoise?

GEAIN: Daughters. Daughters of Darkness.

MERVYN: Oh, those, yes, What about them?

GEAIN: Wouldn't let me in.

MERVYN: Wouldn't let you in? In where? In the shop?

GEAIN: No.

MERVYN: Why ever not?

GEAIN: They hate us. We hate them.

MERVYN: Oh, dear. That's not very friendly, is it?

CORINNA: They're great rivals apparently. Amazing as it may sound, the Sons of Bitches and the Daughters of Darknesses aren't speaking to each other at all.

GEAIN: Rancid sows.

CORINNA: (*To* JEROME) Your son, you will observe, has joined the Male Dominance Movement – the Top Missionaries . . . whatever they're called.

GEAIN: (*Through her sandwich*) The Missionary Position.

CORINNA: Missionary Position.

(*A silence.*)

Well, I've no doubt you two will have lots to talk about. (*Pause.*) Talking of missionaries, shouldn't you call Zoë? She should meet Geain, surely?

MERVYN: Oh, yes. Let's bring Zoë in.

JEROME: (*Still dazed, calling*) Darling!

NAN'S VOICE: (*From the bedroom*) Hallo, darling?

JEROME: Darling, come in. My – my – Geain's arrived.

NAN: (*Off*) Right you are, darling. Just a tick.

CORINNA: Zoë is Dad's new friend, Geain. His fiancée.

(GEAIN *looks at* JEROME *scornfully*. JEROME *looks at* GEAIN *and gives a little despairing moan*.)

GEAIN: Huh!

(NAN *enters from the bedroom*.)

NAN: (*Brightly, as she enters*) Hallo! Hallo! Hallo! Welcome! Welcome! Welcome! Sorry. I completely lost tra–

76

CORINNA: This is Geain, Zoë. Geain, say hallo to Zoë.
(GEAIN *stares at* NAN. NAN *stares at* GEAIN. *For various reasons, neither of them speaks.*)
Ah. (*Softly*) Geain, at least say hallo.

GEAIN: 'llo.

JEROME: (*Rather automatically*) Darling. This is Geain. Treasure.

NAN: (*At once*) Well, who's this beautiful little girl, then? You must be Geain, mustn't you? Well, Geain, I'm Zoë. And we're going to be very, very good friends, aren't we? I hope we are. Now would you like to come into the kitchen with me and I'll give you a big glass of orange, how about that? Come on, then, come with Zoë . . .

GEAIN: (*Backing away from* NAN's *outstretched hand*) Get off. Get her off me.

NAN: Off we go. I've got a big surprise for you out here, Geain.
(*Before anyone can stop them,* NAN *has dragged the protesting* GEAIN *off to the kitchen.*)

CORINNA: (*Somewhat alarmed*) Geain won't drink orange juice, Jerome . . .

JEROME: Hang on, I'll stop her, I'll . . .
(*He makes to follow them.*)

MERVYN: (*Quite forcefully, for him*) No, no, no, no, no.
(JEROME *stops.*)

JEROME: What?

MERVYN: Leave them together. Please. The very best thing that can happen. A chance for them to get to know each other.

JEROME: Yes, but – she wasn't supposed to do all that – she –

MERVYN: Please. Trust my judgement. I am trained in these matters.

CORINNA: She'll never get Geain to drink orange juice, I can tell you that.

MERVYN: Then they will no doubt resolve matters between them. Geain will tell Zoë no, thank you, Zoë, I do not want orange juice, thank you very much indeed, I would like a glass of milk. Or somesuch.

CORINNA: Or somesuch.

MERVYN: And Zoë will no doubt defer to Geain's request and

give her what she wants –

JEROME: Possibly.

MERVYN: And that way a bond will be formed between them. We call that, in my line of work, a Self-Seeding Relationship.

(*There is a crash from the kitchen.*)

NAN: (*Off*) Oh, for goodness' sake, you extremely stupid old bat. Who put that there, then?

(JEROME *makes to go off again.*)

JEROME: I'd better just go and –

MERVYN: No, no, no. Please, please, Mr Watkins. Trust me.

JEROME: It's just, you see, that Zoë isn't –

MERVYN: No, I appreciate that. Zoë is not used to youngsters and she'll have to learn as she goes. No doubt she'll make mistakes. Being human, it would be extraordinary if she didn't.

JEROME: It would.

MERVYN: But what's happening out there is a mutual exploration process. Now, please. Leave them to explore each other. Let's all sit down, keep calm and allow nature to take its course.

(*They sit. A silence. A crash.*)

CORINNA: Jerome, she'll kill her. If you leave them together, she'll kill her.

MERVYN: Oh, come now –

CORINNA: Well, we could at least listen to them, couldn't we? See they're all right? I take it the rooms are still wired for sound? Did you know, Mr Bickerdyke, he records everything? Be careful. When Geain and I lived here – every word, every breath we took was recorded and played back to us.

JEROME: Nonsense.

CORINNA: It's true.

JEROME: I never played half of it back to you.

MERVYN: (*Who has been listening more towards the kitchen*) They seem very quiet now. I'm sure things are going to be fine. We mustn't expect results straightaway but – it's a start.

CORINNA: I still don't think she should be left out there alone

78

with her . . .

JEROME: I don't know. Maybe it's all right. Zoë's – very gentle . . .

CORINNA: I'm talking about Geain. Nobody tells Geain what to drink. I've still got this bruise where she kicked me because I bought the wrong biscuits.

JEROME: I hope she doesn't try and kick Zoë.

CORINNA: Yes, she's turned into a right little thug, your daughter. First suggestion she isn't going to get her own way, she punches and kicks. Good luck. That's all I can say. Maybe you'll have more success with your child than I have . .

(*Another crash from the kitchen.*)

JEROME: Let me get one thing clear. That – thing in there is no relation of mine – that transvestite truck driver . . .

MERVYN: Mr Watkins –

JEROME: (*With a cry*) What have you done with my little girl? I want my little girl. I've never seen that thing before. (*Yelling at* CORINNA) What is it? I don't want that. Take it away! Screw it back on the church roof where it belongs . . .

MERVYN: Mr Watkins, will you please control yourself? (JEROME *is silent.*)

CORINNA: It's all right, Mr Bickerdyke, I'm accustomed to these outbursts, believe me. In reply to your question, Jerome, I have done nothing – because there was nothing that I or anyone else could do. Geain does what Geain likes and stuff the rest of the world. I can't think who she – sorry he – inherits that particularly unpleasant side of his nature from, so we can only hazard a guess. But he – she – *it* does what it likes. *It* goes to school, *it* has friends, *it* wants to be like *its* friends. If its friends choose to dress up like that, I can't stop it. Because, as it explains to me, if it doesn't dress up like its friends then it won't have any friends any more. I have to admit that it's not a great deal of fun having a female male chauvinist kicking me all day, demanding to be waited on hand and foot and referring to me as a dozy cow. But looking at some of the alternatives it

79

might have chosen, I've decided to grin and bear it. Now if you want to try and alter her, you're welcome to try. Go ahead. Please. Because I really do need help, Jerome. I can't do it alone. I really believed, after I left you, that I could cope with anything. I was wrong. I cannot cope with Geain as she is now. Maybe in a few years, when she's . . . There you are, I admit it. And I am shocked by my own inadequacy. I am even a little ashamed. It's made a trifle more bearable because I'm absolutely certain that nobody else, in these circumstances, could have coped any better than I did.

MERVYN: (*Gently*) I'm sure you've done everything that a single parent could, Corinna.

(*A brief silence.*)

It's very quiet out there, isn't it?

(*Before they can move,* NAN *comes back from the kitchen. She waits by the doorway.*)

NAN: Here she is, Mummy. Here she is, Daddy.

(GEAIN *comes in slowly from the kitchen. She looks slightly dazed. Her face is now clean, almost gleaming. She has on a too-long nightdress. She carries a large frilly doll in her arms.*)

JEROME: (*Muttering*) Oh, my God . . .

CORINNA: (*Stunned*) Geain!

MERVYN: Well . . .

NAN: And what are we going to sing, Geain?

(GEAIN *scowls.*)

Geain. (*Prompting her*) 'Baa baa . . .'

GEAIN: I'm not saying that . . .

NAN: All together.

Baa baa black sheep, whither do you wander?

Four and twenty blackbirds baked on a tuffet – good –

The little dog laughed to see such fun

And said what a good boy am I. Woof! Moo! Well done.

(NAN *claps. The others follow suit in a perplexed manner.*)

GEAIN: (*Not without admiration*) She's mad.

MERVYN: That's a new one on me, certainly.

(*He laughs.*)

NAN: (*Laughing, taking hold of* GEAIN's *hand*) Now we're off to

80

bed. Goodnight, everyone. Say goodnight.

GEAIN: I'm not saying goodnight.

NAN: (*Dragging her away*) That's it.

GEAIN: (*Struggling vainly as they go*) I can't go to bed now, you dumb woman . . .

(*They go off to the bedrooms. A cry from* GEAIN.)

NAN: (*Off*) Oh, for goodness' sake, you extremely stupid old bat. Who put that there, then?

(*They stare at each other.*)

MERVYN: Well, I must say. In all my years, I've – What a remarkable woman. Quite remarkable.

(JEROME *is aware that* CORINNA *is quite upset.*)

JEROME: Well, it's – it's just part of her – basic – original – I mean it was there already in her, you see . . .

MERVYN: As it is within all women, Mr Watkins. All women. (*A pause.*) Well, that's a problem solved.

CORINNA: Would you think it terribly rude of me, Mr Bickerdyke, if I were to ask you to leave us alone for a moment?

MERVYN: Ah, well . . .

CORINNA: Actually, I don't really care if you do find it terribly rude of me. Would you go, anyway.

MERVYN: (*Springing up*) Yes, of course. I'll – I'll wait in the – (*Indicating the kitchen.*)

JEROME: The kitchen.

MERVYN: I'll wait in there, shall I? I have to phone my – Yes. Excuse me. (*He takes a handful of sandwiches as he goes.*) Excuse me.

(MERVYN *goes to the kitchen.* CORINNA *and* JEROME *are silent for a second.*)

CORINNA: All I want to say is – I think I'll leave now. Quietly. I'll leave Geain with you and Zoë. All right?

JEROME: Ah.

CORINNA: Well, that's what you'd like, isn't it? That's what you wanted?

JEROME: Yes.

CORINNA: I mean obviously she'll have to return to me – at some point – she has to go back to school for one thing.

81

But she could stay here for a couple of weeks, anyway. See how it works out.

JEROME: You're happy to do that? You think that's best?

CORINNA: Frankly, Jerome, I feel so demoralized I don't know what I think. All I actually feel like doing is crying. I mean, that woman's done more with that kid in five minutes than I managed in five years.

JEROME: That's just her being a stranger, she –

CORINNA: I might have been able to cope with that, if Zoë'd at least been – terribly plain or – homely – or . . . I thought for one glorious moment she was actually very dim. But then, of course, it turns out she isn't. She's obviously very intelligent, shrewd, cool, sexy, wonderful with kids, a great actress, singer, dancer, terrific in bed – the only thing she lies about are her cakes – and it's bloody unfair, Jerome. (*She starts to cry.*)

JEROME: Oh now, come on –

CORINNA: How can it be allowed to happen? After all you've done? All the rotten, traitorous, lousy, underhand things you've done to me. What right have you to somebody like that? You're a bastard, Jerome. You're barely human. What have you ever done in your life to deserve *anyone*?

JEROME: Well, I can't answer that . . . I really can't.

CORINNA: There is no justice. That's all. None. Here's me – (*She sniffs.*) I haven't found anyone, do you know that? Nobody.

JEROME: Ah, that's only because you have very high standards. Quite rightly . . .

CORINNA: I've got no standards at all. Not any more. I'll take anyone who's available. I'm a forty-year-old bank manager who sits crying in her office. What use is that to anybody? Do you know I gave a man a loan the other day solely on the grounds that I wanted to go to bed with him?

JEROME: My God. And did you?

CORINNA: Of course I didn't. I found out he only borrowed the money so he could get married. I'm losing my judgement, I'm losing my confidence and then that bloody child comes home from school and kicks me because of a packet of

82

biscuits. I can't cope any more. I just want to go somewhere and lie down.

(JEROME *stares at her, amazed*.)

(*Amused, despite herself, by his expression*) There! I bet you never thought you'd hear me talking like this. (*Pause*.) How did she get Geain to *wash*? I never got her to wash. She stank to high heaven. Sweat is macho. Well. Tell Zoë to keep up the good work. I'll collect the exciting Mr Bickerdyke and slink away.

JEROME: Yes. Well, you never know your luck, you may –

CORINNA: Don't you dare. Don't even suggest it. I have a fragment of pride left. Well, cheer up. You're not allowed to be miserable. You've got what you wanted, haven't you?

JEROME: Yes.

CORINNA: As you usually do. (*Pause*.) I'll tell you something amusing, shall I? You know, half the reason I came here was to see how you felt about – felt about, you know, coming back.

JEROME: Coming back?

CORINNA: Yes, I – well, when I thought you were still on your own here, I thought that we might all three get together. Have another go. But I didn't know about Zoë, of course. Now she's staked her claim, I don't think I could compete with that. Not the state I'm in at present. (*Pause*.) Still, I thought that would amuse you.

(*Pause. She rises*.)

JEROME: (*Slowly*) Just a second . . .

CORINNA: I'll call Mr Bickerdyke.

JEROME: Wait . . .

CORINNA: I don't think there's much else to say, Jerome.

JEROME: There's something I need to tell you. Please.

CORINNA: No, I don't want to hear about –

JEROME: No, you see, things are not – altogether as they seem. The reason Zoë is here at all is because – I needed someone here – to impress you.

CORINNA: Well, she did, well done.

JEROME: No, that's the only reason she's here, you see, so that you and Mr Bickerdyke – so you'd let Geain stay here.

83

Because it looked OK.

CORINNA: What exactly are you saying? Are you saying that Zoë is only here for our benefit?

JEROME: Yes.

CORINNA: She isn't here normally?

JEROME: No.

CORINNA: Then who is she?

JEROME: She's – she's an actress. She really is an actress. This is just a – short engagement. So to speak.

CORINNA: What did you do, hire her?

JEROME: Right.

CORINNA: (*Staring at him*) I see. I see.

(*She is exercising a great effort of self-control.*)

JEROME: (*Watching her, apprehensively*) So that's OK, then, isn't it? I mean, now you don't have to be upset. Do you? You don't need to feel jealous of Zoë. Or – or inadequate. Or unattractive. She's just an actress – who – who looks good and can handle children. But she's nothing compared with you. I mean, if you'd only said you – you wanted us to – Well, that's great. You know, that's what I wanted? Isn't that amazing? That's exactly what I wanted. There we were, the two of us – both wanting the same thing – and . . . Isn't life sometimes little short of miraculous? (*Pause.*) Alleluiah!

CORINNA: (*Icily*) I hope you're recording all of this, Jerome. You'll no doubt have such a good laugh playing it back to yourself later. (*Calling*) Mr Bickerdyke.

JEROME: What the hell's the matter, now?

CORINNA: Mr Bickerdyke!

(MERVYN *returns from the kitchen. He is putting away his phone.*)

MERVYN: Coming. Just talking to the wife. We're having a dinner party tonight. My big chief is coming. With her husband. My wife reckons my chief is after me for bigger things. I said to my wife, I don't care what she's after so long as it isn't my body.

(*He laughs.*)

CORINNA: (*Frostily*) We're just leaving, Mr Bickerdyke.

84

MERVYN: When you're ready. All settled?

JEROME: Leaving? I thought –

CORINNA: I'll just fetch Geain. She must get dressed. (*Calling as she goes*) Geain!

MERVYN: Geain! But I thought . . .

(CORINNA *goes off towards the bedrooms*.)

What's happening? I thought Geain was staying.

JEROME: Yes. Things seem to have . . . changed. Something seems to have caused Corinna to change her mind.

MERVYN: Yes? Well – strictly between us, Mr Watkins – your ex-wife appears to me to be a woman operating under some considerable inner stress.

JEROME: Yes?

MERVYN: Not, if you'll pardon my humour, quite the woman you'd want to see handling your investments.

(*He laughs*.)

(CORINNA *returns*.)

CORINNA: Right. I've called her.

MERVYN: What's caused the change of plan, may I inquire?

CORINNA: I'm afraid, Mr Bickerdyke, we've both been the victim of one of my husband's practical jokes.

MERVYN: We have?

CORINNA: Zoë is not what she appears. She was merely rented by Jerome for the afternoon. She doesn't belong here and she doesn't live here.

MERVYN: But why – ? (*To* JEROME) Why did you do that?

CORINNA: To deceive you, Mr Bickerdyke, and to make a fool of me. That's why.

JEROME: That is not why I did it –

CORINNA: (*Calling*) Geain! If we leave now, Jerome, you can send your actress home early. You may even get some of your money back. I presume she's rented by the hour.

JEROME: I don't understand you. I thought you'd be pleased.

CORINNA: Delighted. Thank you so much.

MERVYN: I don't follow this? I don't follow this at all.

(GEAIN *appears, still in her 'nightdress', holding* NAN'*s hand. They stop in the doorway*.)

CORINNA: Come along, Geain, there's been a slight confusion,

85

we're going home.

JEROME: Just a second, just a second . . .

MERVYN: Now, let me get this straight. Are we saying that this woman, that Zoë is not living here with you? She is not a permanent companion but someone you have rented . . . ?

JEROME: I don't see that the terms on which she's staying here make the blindest bit of difference, anyway.

MERVYN: No difference?

JEROME: Either she's suitable or she isn't suitable. It doesn't make any difference whether I'm paying her.

MERVYN: I hardly think that argument holds water –

CORINNA: Of course it doesn't. Don't waste your breath. Come on.

MERVYN: I mean, you may as well say there's no difference between a legal wife and a prostitute – I don't think I can accept that argument . . .

JEROME: Let me tell you that that – that woman (*Waves his hand in* NAN's *direction*) – has more dignity, more sense of loyalty and responsibility than any other fifty women you can name put together . . .

CORINNA: You? What do you know about women . . . ?

JEROME: (*To* MERVYN) Anyway, what's made you change your mind all of a sudden? You liked her well enough –

MERVYN: Ah, yes, but this was before I'd heard . . .

JEROME: Couldn't keep your eyes off her, could you? Ogling and leering at her, your mouth stuffed with cake, you grubby little berk . . .

MERVYN: Now, now, now, now . . .

CORINNA: Will you stop this?

MERVYN: If you think that a remark of that sort will do your case one ounce of good –

JEROME: (*Simultaneously*) If we're having to rely on decisions from people like you, matey, what's it matter anyway? The ship's already sinking.

CORINNA: (*Loudly, silencing them*) Will you shut up, both of you!

(*A silence.*)

Thank you. There is no point in arguing over this. Geain,

86

come along please, we are going home. (*Pause.*) Geain.

GEAIN: No.

CORINNA: What?

GEAIN: I don't want to go.

CORINNA: You don't –

GEAIN: I'm staying here.

JEROME: There you are. There you are, you see. Out of the mouths . . . You heard that, Mr Bickerdyke? My daughter chooses to stay here with me. Could that be clearer?

GEAIN: Son.

JEROME: What?

CORINNA: Son. At least get its sex right.

JEROME: My son, then, has chosen to stay with its father. Its natural father. There is justice. Thank you, God, there is justice.

CORINNA: This you note, Mr Bickerdyke, from a man who a few minutes ago asked to have this transvestite truck driver screwed back on the church roof.

JEROME: That was a joke. That was a joke – between men. Eh, Geain?

CORINNA: Geain, I appreciate that after four years of me, your father probably holds some small novelty appeal. But may I warn you, dear, that it wears very, very thin, very, very rapidly.

JEROME: Don't listen to that, Geain. Ignore this woman's prattle.

MERVYN: May I just – I'm going to have to bound in here, once again . . . Geain. I'm afraid there's no question of your staying here, dear . . .

JEROME: Don't listen to him, either. He's an old woman.

MERVYN: Please, Mr Watkins. So far as I can gather, Geain, that woman whose hand you are holding is someone your father rented – for the day. Zoë is an actress pretending to be a friend of your father's. But she does not belong here and she doesn't intend staying. She is not a woman, therefore, we consider suitable to look after you. Do you understand that, Geain?

GEAIN: She's not a woman.

87

MERVYN: What?

GEAIN: I said she's not a woman.

CORINNA: What do you mean, she's not a woman . . .

GEAIN: She's a machine.

MERVYN: (*Laughing*) Now, come along, Geain, that's rather baby talk for someone of your age, isn't it – ?

GEAIN: She is. (*Indicating* JEROME) Ask him.

MERVYN: Well, I'm sure your father isn't going to – He's certainly not going to – He won't . . . He's not . . . (*He is looking to* JEROME *for a denial but tails off when he doesn't get one.*)

JEROME: Yes, Geain's right. She's a machine.

CORINNA: I have never heard such . . . They're both as mad as each other.

GEAIN: (*Lifting* NAN's *skirt to reveal her metal upper legs*) Look.

CORINNA: (*Screaming*) Oh, dear God.

MERVYN: (*With her*) Wah!

CORINNA: (*In a low voice*) What is it? What have you let near her . . .

JEROME: It's only a – It's just a machine.

CORINNA: But I've never seen – Where did it come from?

JEROME: Er – from the man down the hall, actually.

CORINNA: The man down the hall? What man down what hall? Get it away from her, Jerome.

GEAIN: Him.

CORINNA: Him. Get it away from him.

JEROME: She's only a machine. It's harmless.

MERVYN: But how did you come by this machine, Mr Watkins? I mean, where did it come from originally? I presume you didn't make it yourself?

JEROME: No. This man gave it to me and I just – patched it up, that's all. Got it working again –

CORINNA: Patched it up? You?

JEROME: Yes.

CORINNA: You can't even mend the front door. Get it away from him.

JEROME: She can – He can walk away from it if he wants to. It's perfectly safe.

88

CORINNA: Geain, walk away from it.

GEAIN: I don't want to walk away from it.

MERVYN: You still haven't answered my question. Where did this thing originate?

JEROME: It – it originated in a factory – it was a prototype for a model that never went into full production. The firm went broke. There's no need to worry. That was actually designed to look after children. It's technically an automatic child-minder. So. Geain couldn't be safer. Could he?

MERVYN: (*Suspiciously*) What was the name of this thing?

JEROME: Well, it's a – a NAN 300F. You probably wouldn't have –

MERVYN: Oh yes, I have. I have indeed. I know all about the NAN 300F, thank you very much.

CORINNA: What about them?

MERVYN: My department had to deal with the whole business.

CORINNA: What business?

JEROME: Nothing. There were a few teething troubles –

CORINNA: What sort?

JEROME: Just teething troubles . . .

MERVYN: Yes, I suppose you could term them that. If you call putting a baby in a microwave oven teething troubles –

CORINNA: It did what?

JEROME: Not this one. This one didn't do that.

MERVYN: One of them did, Mr Watkins, one of them did.

CORINNA: It put a baby – ?

JEROME: That was entirely the mother's fault.

MERVYN: The mother's?

JEROME: It wasn't the machine's fault – the mother had her kitchen moved around and never told the machine. I mean, how can you expect a machine to know any better –

MERVYN: I don't see how you can possibly take the side of a machine against a human being.

JEROME: Against most human beings, very easily. If human beings behaved a bit less like human beings and a bit more like machines, we'd all be better off –

MERVYN: That is the most extraordinary argument I have ever

89

heard . . .

CORINNA: Look, would you mind? That thing, that baby-killer, is at present holding my son's hand. Will you please do something about it? Mr Bickerdyke?

MERVYN: Yes, I'll – I'll . . . Right. (*Speaking to* NAN, *slowly and nervously*) Let go. Let go her. Go let!
(*There is no response from* NAN.)

CORINNA: Oh, for heaven's sake. (*Approaching* NAN *determinedly*) Will you let go of my child's hand at once? (*Standing bravely eye to eye with* NAN) Do you hear me?

NAN: I know what you're after, dear, and you're not going to have him. If you want Jerome, the only way you're going to get him is over my dead body, you calculating little trollop.

CORINNA: (*Stepping back*) Oh, dear God . . .

NAN: You'd better watch your step, Mrs Danvers, or one of these nights you're going to wake up with your throat cut.

CORINNA: (*Retreating*) What have you put in this thing, Jerome? Who have you got in there?

JEROME: No, she must have mistaken you for –

CORINNA: I know who she mistook me for, thank you, I'm not a complete fool . . . But who does she imagine she is?

JEROME: (*Intrigued by this question*) I don't know, you know. I never really asked her.

CORINNA: Are you going to tell it to release our child?

JEROME: Not unless our child wants to be released.

CORINNA: How can you let this happen? You heard what he said.

MERVYN: It's all right. Leave this to me. I'll stop this. (*To* NAN) Come on. Or I may have to resort to force.

JEROME: I wouldn't –

MERVYN: (*Approaching* NAN) Come on. You have no right to that child . . .

JEROME: Be careful, she may think you're a child-molester.

MERVYN: I'm certainly not a child-molester, how dare you? (*To* NAN) Come along . . .
(MERVYN *tries to pull* GEAIN *away from* NAN. NAN *grips* MERVYN'*s face in the palm of her hand for a second. Then, with a seemingly effortless push, sends the man reeling back*

90

across the room. MERVYN *trips and falls on to his back.*)

GEAIN: (*Admiringly*) Yeah!

CORINNA: Stop her!

JEROME: Nan!

(*A loud intermittent whooping sound is heard as* MERVYN'S *personal alarm system goes off.*)

CORINNA: What the hell's that?

JEROME: It must be his alarm system.

CORINNA: Well, switch if off. Get him to switch if off. Geain, come along.

GEAIN: No.

CORINNA: It's dangerous. Darling, you saw what it did to Mr Bickerdyke.

GEAIN: Yeah!

NAN: I saw what it did to Mr Bickerdyke, darling.

CORINNA: Oh, dear God. It's mad. It's a mad machine. Will somebody stop that noise?

JEROME: I think he's unconscious.

CORINNA: Well, you do it . . .

JEROME: I don't know if I can. I don't suppose it's designed to –

(JEROME *starts to fumble around under the inert* MERVYN'S *shirt. He comes out with a handful of wire. He pulls it hopefully. Under the next, he unravels several yards of wire from somewhere within the recesses of* MERVYN.)

CORINNA: Just do it. Now, come along, Jerome, how do I get this machine away from Geain? Please.

JEROME: Call it darling. You have to call it that. She's programmed to respond to 'darling'.

CORINNA: Oh, yes? Well, don't count on it as a general principle. (*Approaching* NAN) Darling . . . Hallo. Darling.

NAN: Hallo, darling.

CORINNA: Oh, this is ridiculous . . . Jerome, will you switch that off –

JEROME: (*His hands full of wire*) I'm trying to switch it off.

CORINNA: (*Trying again with* NAN) Let go, darling. Geain, please, sweetheart . . .

NAN: (*Promptly*) I'd love to have children of my own. Wouldn't

91

it be lovely to hear them rushing about the flat, laughing and yelling? With the right man – someone who'd share them – they'd be everything I ever wanted. I suppose you're either maternal or you aren't. I know which I am.

CORINNA: (*Over this*) What is it talking about? Jerome, it's gone completely berserk, it's off again . . .

JEROME: It's OK. You just keep feeding it trigger words, that's all –

CORINNA: What the hell are you talking about, 'trigger words'?
(JEROME *leaves* MERVYN *swathed in wire. He comes over to help* CORINNA. MERVYN, *at this moment, starts to recover.*)

JEROME: Look. You just have to do this, that's all. Darling.

NAN: Yes, darling.

JEROME: Darling, let go.

NAN: Letting go, darling.
(NAN *immediately releases* GEAIN's *hand.*)

GEAIN: (*Promptly retaking* NAN's *hand*) No.

CORINNA: Geain, for goodness' sake . . .
(MERVYN *gets to his knees and reaches with difficulty down the back of his jacket. The alarm stops.*)

MERVYN: It's all right, I'm all right, I . . . (*Aware of the wire that emanates from him*) My God, what's all this? What have you done to me? I'm coming apart.

CORINNA: Oh, do be quiet.

MERVYN: Look at this. What have you done?

JEROME: I'm sorry, I was trying to switch you off.

MERVYN: Well, thank you so much. You've successfully unravelled my Italian thermal singlet. Thank you so very much.

CORINNA: (*Back to* NAN) Darling, let go. Darling, let go.
(NAN *does not respond.*)
Jerome, she's taking no notice of me.

JEROME: No, that's odd.

MERVYN: A hundred and forty-three pounds' worth of imported garment here.

CORINNA: Oh, do shut up about your precious vest.
(NAN *kisses her on the cheek.* CORINNA *leaps back.*)
Get away! Get away!

JEROME: Darling, let go.

(NAN *does not respond.*)

No, I think Geain's overridden her. It's a safety thing. She won't let go unless Geain lets go.

CORINNA: Then, Geain, let go.

GEAIN: No.

MERVYN: All right, I'll deal with this. I'm going downstairs and I'm going to fetch help. I'll bring our friends up from the car. They'll sort it out, don't you worry.

(MERVYN *goes off along the hall. In a moment, we see him go out of the flat on the video screen. He leaves the door open.*)

CORINNA: Well, what are we going to do? Eh?

JEROME: There's nothing we can do. If she won't let go, she won't let go.

CORINNA: Geain, listen to me . . .

GEAIN: I'm not letting go.

CORINNA: Why not?

GEAIN: I don't want to.

CORINNA: But. That's a machine. You can't stay with a machine, can you?

GEAIN: Why not?

CORINNA: Because – because it's a machine –

GEAIN: Dad did.

CORINNA: Yes. Well, your father's – Your father's your father. But ordinary people . . . like us – we can't stay – (*She gives up.*) Jerome, for God's sake, tell her.

JEROME: (*Unconvincingly*) Yes. Geain. You see, you can't stay with a machine, can you – ?

GEAIN: Why not?

JEROME: Because. Human beings are – better. They're far – superior to machines because . . .

GEAIN: Why . . .

JEROME: Because human beings are . . . they're . . .

(*He pauses.*)

CORINNA: (*Impatiently*) For God's sake, Jerome! Tell her why they're better –

JEROME: (*Desperately*) I can't think of a reason! Not a single one! I think she's right.

93

CORINNA: She's not right. You are not right, Geain. And
neither is he. Listen. In the past, your father and I, we
have – we have both been selfish, we have been thoughtless
and stupid and – human. But we have also been, in our
time, warm and spontaneous and amusing and joyful and –
loving. Which is something we can also be, because we are
human. But which that machine can never be. You see?
(GEAIN *seems to be still waiting to be convinced.*)
What we are going to do now, the three of us – you, me
and Jerome – we are going down to that car and we are
driving home together. And we're all going to start again.
All of us. As of now. Isn't that right, Jerome? Jerome?

JEROME: Right now? This minute?

CORINNA: Yes.

JEROME: What about all this gear, I can't just . . . ?

CORINNA: Jerome, get this straight. It is us – or your gear. It is
this thing – (*Indicating* NAN) – or us. Decide.
(*A brief pause.*)

JEROME: Yes. OK.

CORINNA: (*Irritably*) Well, which is it to be?

JEROME: (*Moving to her*) You. Of course, you.

CORINNA: All right. Then, that's it. Geain? Will you let go
now? Are you coming with us?

GEAIN: (*Finally releasing* NAN) OK.
(*She moves to* CORINNA *and* JEROME. *The three embrace.*)

CORINNA: Thank God.
(MERVYN *appears on the video screen hurrying back into the
flat.*)
Right. Change your clothes, we'll get in the car.

GEAIN: Yeah.
(*She is about to go off to fetch her clothes from the kitchen
when* MERVYN *rushes in.*)

CORINNA: It's all right . . .

MERVYN: No, it is not all right. We are under seige.

JEROME: What?

MERVYN: Those Daughters – whatever they call themselves.
They're swarming all over the place outside. Our two are
only just managing to hold them off. We have to leave now.

94

GEAIN: Rancid sows.

CORINNA: Oh, dear Lord. Geain, come as you are. You haven't got time to change now.

(*A clang as a missile hits one of the shutters.*)

MERVYN: We do have to hurry.

CORINNA: Tell them we're coming, tell them we're on our way.

MERVYN: Quick as you can.

(*Another missile.*)

CORINNA: Geain . . .

GEAIN: Right. (*To* NAN) Cheerio then. (*To* JEROME) Can Zoë say goodbye to me?

CORINNA: Geain, do come on.

GEAIN: I want Zoë to say goodbye to me.

JEROME: Darling. Say goodbye to Geain.

NAN: Goodbye, Geain, dear. See you soon. See you very soon.

(*She waves.*) Bye-bye. Bye-bye.

GEAIN: Bye, Zoë. See you again.

CORINNA: No, darling, you won't be seeing her again, I'm afraid. Sorry about that. Goodbye.

(NAN *stops waving. More missiles hit the shutters.*)

All right. Jerome?

JEROME: I'm coming, I'll just fetch a few . . .

GEAIN: Come on, Dad.

JEROME: Yes, I will. I promise. You go on.

CORINNA: They won't wait.

(CORINNA *and* GEAIN *go out down the hall. We see them on the screen leaving the flat. The door remains open. The screen is left lit.* JEROME *goes off to the bedroom.* NAN *is left alone. In a moment, she moves and sits in the chair. A silence. Then, the same technician's voice that we heard at the start emanates from somewhere within* NAN. *Her lips move vaguely in sync.*)

VOICE: NAN 300F, series four, model 99148622G for Gertie. Function now completed. System final closedown – in two minutes. Safety count commencing at sixty seconds.

(NAN *sits very still, swaying slightly as she sings softly to herself.*)

NAN: (*Sings:*) You're not my first love . . .

It would only be a lie if I pretended –

95

In the past there have been others
Who have slept between these covers
But I promise
Though you're far too late in life to be my first love,
You'll be my last love.
I swear to you, you're gonna be my last love . . .

(*As she sings,* JEROME *comes back with a hastily packed holdall. He gives* NAN *the merest of glances. Another missile hits the shutters.* JEROME *goes to the console. He seems to be deliberating what to take with him. He stands undecided.* CORINNA *appears on the screen as she re-enters the flat. A moment later, she comes in from the hall.*)

CORINNA: Jerome, what are you doing?

JEROME: Sorry, I was just –

CORINNA: They're swarming around out there. There's dozens of them. They're trying to get at Geain. I told her not to come dressed like that. Are you coming?

JEROME: Listen, when you –

CORINNA: (*Impatient*) What?

JEROME: When you said all that about us – restarting – was that just to get Geain to leave or –

CORINNA: No, of course it wasn't. I wouldn't have said it for that.

JEROME: You sure?

CORINNA: Yes.

JEROME: You want me back with you?

CORINNA: Yes.

JEROME: Why?

CORINNA: (*Desperately, at the end of her tether*) Because we both love you, Jerome. God knows why, but we love you. Love, love, love! All right. Now, come on, please.

JEROME: I will. I'm coming. Go ahead. Tell them I'm on my way. (*He kisses her.*)
Go on. Don't let them leave.

CORINNA: Be quick.

(CORINNA *goes out. We see her leave once more on the screen.* JEROME *grabs up a tape, the one of* GEAIN. *He goes out after her.*)

96

VOICE: (*From* NAN) Safety count commencing. Sixty – fifty-nine – fifty-eight – fifty-seven – fifty-six – fifty-five . . .
(*As the count continues, the* VOICE *slowly gets quieter and quieter until only her lips are moving.* JEROME *appears on the screen at the front door. He seems about to leave, changes his mind and comes back into the flat, this time closing the front door.* NAN'*s count continues. So does the sound of missiles striking the shutters with increasing regularity.* JEROME *returns and goes to the console. He stops the recording machine and winds it back.*)

JEROME'S RECORDED VOICE: . . . about us – restarting – was that just to persuade Geain to leave or –

CORINNA'S RECORDED VOICE: No, of cours–
(JEROME *spools forward again. He replays.*)
. . . both love you, Jerome. God knows why, but we love you. Love, love, love! Alri–
(JEROME *plays around with the recording some more.* NAN *continues in silence, her mouth barely moving.*)
Love! Love! Love! . . .

JEROME: (*Like a man who has had a vision*) My God!
(*He rushes round the room uncovering the rest of the technical equipment that, till now, has remained unseen. Nearly everything in the room, it transpires, is actually part of* JEROME'*s recording and sampling gear, including the coffee table. As he does this, a fresh series of furious clangs are heard on the shutters outside. These he all but ignores. While he does this,* NAN'*s countdown reaches zero and she shuts down. Quietly and with very little sign. She lifts one hand slightly and then lets it drop. A final wave. Her head slumps and she goes limp.* JEROME *begins to work feverishly now, treating the original sound of* CORINNA'*s cry of 'love', sampling and synthesizing. A whole complex, interminable process, dramatically condensed into stage seconds.* JEROME *starts to play. At first improvising, then slowly growing in confidence as he goes, the texture ever thickening, building in volume. A great chorus of varying 'love's – all stemming from* CORINNA'*s original. This is his 'love' composition. He plays for perhaps three or four minutes. During* JEROME'*s playing the doorbell*

97

must have rung unheard because the screen is filled with the faces of CORINNA, GEAIN *and* MERVYN *all silently shouting at the video camera outside to be readmitted. This is swiftly interrupted by the image of* LUPUS *appearing on the screen – apparently the phone has rung, too.* JEROME *fails to notice any of it.* LUPUS *is on some sort of hospital trolley – evidently on his way for surgery. He is swathed in bandages and is only barely recognizable. But his spirit, beneath all that, seems reasonably unimpaired. He waves his arms, talking animatedly, if inaudibly. He shows* JEROME *his one unbandaged thumb in a thumbs-up sign, as always reassuring his friend not to worry about him.* LUPUS *is slowly wheeled away from the camera, up the corridor. This image is cross-cut with increasing speed as* CORINNA's, GEAIN's *and* MERVYN's *images momentarily override the incoming video call. Finally, a nurse's hand switches off the hospital picture. On screen, at the front door,* CORINNA *and company take a final look behind them and rush away.* RITA, *the Daughter of Darkness, yelling inaudible obscenities, comes racing up the hall brandishing an iron bar. Noticing the camera in passing, she pauses to smash it. The screen goes dark.* JEROME, *oblivious, plays on like a man possessed. Finally, with a great flourish, he finishes. A silence. He stands, triumphant.*)
(*Jubilant and breathless*) That's it! That's *it!*
(*A silence. A missile, thrown from outside, clangs against the shutters.* JEROME *does not react.*)
(*Already feeling rather anti-climactic*) That's it. (*He looks around him and sits.*) Yeah! (*Pause.*) That's it, then.
(*He sits all alone. And realizes how alone he is. As the missiles continue to clang – curtain.*)

98